THE
SURE
MERCIES
OF DAVID

THE SURE MERCIES OF DAVID
© 2007 by Al and Jayne Houghton

Printed in the United States of America

Published by
Word At Work Ministries, Inc.
P.O. Box 366   Placentia, California 92871   USA

www.wordatwork.org

ISBN 978-0-940252-07-3

THE SURE MERCIES OF DAVID

Al Houghton

This book is dedicated to
Pastors John and Ruth Ann Cairns
and
Pastors Noel and Phyllis Weiss.

For Jayne and I in our formative years,
they were mentors who mastered
mercy as a way of life!

ACKNOWLEDGEMENTS

The message of this book started as a Holy Spirit posed question in Stuttgart, Germany. It has been road tested from Anchorage to Atlanta and Honolulu to Halifax. The manuscript was submitted to a collegial cross-section of Christianity for criticism from coast to coast

Jayne and I wish to thank: Pastor Larry Brewer for his very thoughtful technical and organizational input; Shan Gastineau for his grasp of Greek and sense of New Testament historical application; Pastor John Schmeling for implementing these principles so quickly with his fellowship and proving their profit; Pat and Gene Gastineau for pioneering in intercession with those who experienced these truths before having a theology for them; Pastor Connie Duffy for the pastoral warning preceding Part II and her insight into the restoration process; Pastor Gayle Homan whose evangelistic heart consistently rises to new heights in encouraging the prophetic; Rev Michael Granum who immersed himself in this manuscript and offered a thousand options; Jo Lees for weeks and months of inserting corrections and changes; Leigh Buckmaster for her excellent and speedy technical editorial skills and finally Sid Roth whose wisdom is responsible for this being one book instead of two.

Table Of Contents

Preface

The end-time church is experiencing a resurrection of the Davidic heart. God gave David a covenant promising to redeem his failures by turning them into a platform for prophetic fulfillment. Isaiah extended this covenant to all who would come and Jesus ratified it with His blood.

The covenant of "Sure Mercy" offers all who would embrace it a two-edged sword. The first edge cuts away condemnation, accusation, shame, and guilt cultivating a covenantal culture of confidence for convening in the Throne Room. The second edge is best viewed as applied in the lives of David and his "mighty men" as they warred to build a godly nation.

No enemy could stand against the anointing they birthed. The Judge of all the earth heard and answered their cries. God went to war in their behalf and "cut off" all their enemies. The covenant of "Sure Mercy" invites us to move God's hand, cutting off the enemy.

"Ask of me, and I will give you the nations . . ." is a promise to be viewed by those with Davidic hearts who know their "Covenant of Sure Mercy" and begin to act on it! This book outlines a "Spiritual Boot Camp" for those who desire to impact nations!

Introduction

As we approach the culmination of the ages, representing Jesus in the end-times is for the church an awesome and amazing assignment. In many ways, the church should be commended for displaying the heart and soul of Jesus in the gospels for many decades. Psalm 2 promises nations as an inheritance for a great end–time harvest, while Revelation outlines a variety and increase of judgments for those choosing to reject God and His ways. The challenge for the church is to walk in both worlds.

The sure mercies of David bring an understanding which empowers both streams of Jesus' ministry. The covenantal care of "Sure Mercy" promises redemption for our failures by transforming them into a platform for our greatest success. As we gain proficiency in redeeming failure, God promises in Isaiah 55 that nations will run to us. Possessing the nations promised by Psalm 2 demands a message of redemption—"Sure Mercy" is that message.

The Jesus of Revelation, however, demands an entirely different preparation in order to give an accurate representation, because He manifests judgment. Revelation 1:16 pictures Jesus with a two–edged sword proceeding out of His mouth. In Revelation 2, addressing the compromising church of Pergamos, He has the two–edged sword and threatens to use it in verse 16: *"Repent, or else I will come to you quickly and will fight against them with the sword of My mouth."*

The first edge of "Sure Mercy" brings covenantal redemption but the second edge is strictly judgment. David understood covenantal mercy meant judgment to the enemy. He specifically prayed, prophesied, and proclaimed covenantal judgment in the Psalms. We cannot display a heart like David without entering this realm! "Sure Mercy" is a two–edged sword!

This book is about using that two–edged sword. The first edge, described in the first twelve chapters, is used to cut away guilt, shame, inadequacy, and condemnation until we can boldly stand with confidence in the Throne Room, accepting and dispensing forgiveness. Only then can we move God's hand to swing the second edge. A church incapable of swinging a two–edged sword is a church unprepared to accurately represent Jesus as Savior and Judge.

Jesus warned us about losing our salt. In some ways, the church has lost its salt! This book is about Kingdom mercy and the Davidic covenant upon which it is based. Confidently using God's two–edged sword and reclaiming our divine salt are end–time essentials. Through covenant, David transformed the outcasts of Israel into an invincible army. This work is dedicated to training a new generation of warriors to extend the Kingdom through redemption and judgment! May the church grow into the fullness that God intends and desires for us to demonstrate. As in the Davidic pattern, the covenant of "Sure Mercy" invites outcasts to become "mighty men" who change nations.

Part I

Sure Mercies

Restoring Failures

Chapter 1

Getting to *Know* the Lord

I see a threefold cord emerging to wind up the age for the generation who chooses to agree with God and accept it! The end–time
church inherits a wealth of blessing, beginning with a reservoir of
unfulfilled intercessions accumulated over many generations. This
is the first cord. Unfulfilled prophetic promises of equal weight rise
before God's Throne demanding divine action, forming the second
strand. One such prophetic promise, pointing to a victorious church,
comes from Daniel 11:32. It says, *"Those who do wickedly against the
covenant he shall corrupt with flattery; but the people who **know** their
God shall be strong, and carry out great exploits."* Amos 9:13 promises
such a great harvest that sowing and growing cycles merge together,
"'Behold, the days are coming' says the LORD, *'When the plowman shall
overtake the reaper, And the treader of grapes him who sows seed; The
mountains shall drip with sweet wine, And all the hills shall flow with
it.'"* Those who are willing to embrace the promises and add their
agreement contribute a third strand, forming a threefold cord that
cannot be easily broken.

Isaiah prophesied about such a church in 60:1–5:

Arise, shine; For your light has come! And the glory of the LORD is risen upon you. For behold, the darkness shall cover the earth, And deep darkness the people; But the LORD will arise over you, And His glory will be seen upon you. The Gentiles shall come to your light, And kings to the brightness of your rising. Lift up your eyes all around, and see: They all gather together, they come to you; Your sons shall come from afar, And your daughters shall be nursed at your side. Then you shall see and become radiant, And your heart shall swell with joy; Because the abundance of the sea shall be turned to you, The wealth of the Gentiles shall come to you.

The prophets agree about an awesome end–time season for those who know God! The largest limiting factor here is a hundred years of preaching Jesus the Savior, primarily to the exclusion of Jesus the Judge. We have arrived at the end of the age with the church knowing one–half of God, because those of us who teach, like Jesus said in Matthew 23, have neglected the weightier half.

The real issue is "knowing" God's fullness in the Hebrew sense. "Know" comes from the Hebrew word *yaw-dah* which means, according to <u>Lexical Aids to the Old Testament,</u> "To perceive, to understand, to acquire knowledge, to know, to discern; to be acquainted with; be known; to make one's self known, to appear; to cause to know; to be familiar, to be aware of; to inform; pronounce; to reveal one's self; to appoint to order."[1]

This is one of the most important Hebrew roots in the entire Old Testament. It occurs 944 times, expressing a broad variety of meanings on various levels of intimacy as we grow to know God.

---

1. *Hebrew–Greek Key Study Bible,* "Lexical Aids to the Old Testament" by Spiros Zodhiates. © 1984. AMG Publishers (Grand Rapids, Michigan). Used by permission.

When this word is applied to a husband and wife, it speaks of the ultimate level of intimacy. But when it is applied to God, the definition broadens to include experience or the track record or path of knowing by failing and experiencing redemption. To take this concept and apply it in a New Testament setting, we must choose to develop intimacy with the Holy Spirit. This intimacy becomes the chief qualifier in birthing an anointing for *"great exploits."* The Spirit and the Word require equal time. Both ingredients fertilize the soil from which grow vessels *"fit for the Master's use."*

First John 3:21 says, *"Beloved, if our heart does not condemn us, we have confidence toward God."* Confidence before God is the fruit of a process which releases us from shame, guilt, and condemnation. If we find ourselves among a very large group who wish they could go back in time and rectify some very costly choices, then accepting God's plan for redeeming us instead holds the key to becoming a warrior like David. Knowing God as redeemer of failure dissolves condemnation and shame, enabling us to confidently walk with Jesus the Judge.

God offers us a covenant which redeems failure! Are we willing to accept that redemption? Moses, David, and Paul share a very common thread of leadership development. All three had major failures that God redeemed and later used as a foundation for ultimately achieving their greatest victories. Their failures became their foundational motivation to press through adversity and accomplish God's call!

Acts 7 records Stephen's defense. Jesus had promised the Holy Spirit would give each person what they needed to answer when summoned before a counsel. Some of what Stephen was given about Moses can't be found anywhere else in Scripture. Verse 22 states, *"And Moses was learned in all the wisdom of the Egyptians, and was mighty in words and deeds."* Many commentaries have suggested Moses had a speech impediment, but that fades rapidly in the light of verse 22.

In verses 23–24 we're told, *"But when he was forty years old, it came into his heart to visit his brethren, the children of Israel. And seeing one of them suffer wrong, he defended and avenged him who was oppressed, and struck down the Egyptian."* At age forty, Moses discovered his call and assumed other Israelites would discern accordingly. Verse 25 says, *"For he supposed that his brethren would have understood that God would deliver them by his hand, but they did not understand. . . ."* In verses 26–27 Moses attempted to move in his call by self–effort, assuming he could bring God's purpose to pass through his own ability. That assumption cost forty more years of preparation! When he had brought Israel out of Egypt, and was called up to the mountain to meet with God, the people got caught moving in the same spirit. They prevailed upon Aaron to fashion a calf and began to party. God was so mad, He wanted to destroy all the people and Aaron according to Exodus 32:11–12:

> Then Moses pleaded with the LORD his God, and said: "LORD, why does Your wrath burn hot against Your people whom You have brought out of the land of Egypt with great power and with a mighty hand? Why should the Egyptians speak, and say, 'He brought them out to harm them, to kill them in the mountains, and to consume them from the face of the earth'"? Turn from Your fierce wrath, and relent from this harm to Your people.

Deuteronomy 9:18–20 amplifies:

> And I fell down before the LORD, as at the first, forty days and forty nights; I neither ate bread nor drank water, because of all your sin which you committed in doing wickedly in the sight of the LORD, to provoke Him to anger. For I was afraid of the anger and hot displeasure with which the LORD was angry with you, to destroy you. But the LORD listened to me at that time also. And

the LORD was very angry with Aaron and would have destroyed him; so I prayed for Aaron also at the same time.

What motivated Moses to spend forty days and nights without food or water to save a nation? One of the major reasons has to be his identification with the fruit of self–effort.

Moses could easily remember his own assumption and motivations at age forty. God redeemed Moses' failure by forgiving him and transforming the sin into motivation to stand in the gap, saving Aaron and the nation! What God did for Moses became a biblical pattern of redemption.

David's greatest failure was adultery with Bathsheba and murdering her husband Uriah to cover the pregnancy. David repented and accepted the eight–step plan of restoration, proving his sincerity. God accepted his repentance and redeemed his failure by bringing the wisest man who ever lived out of a union that began in adultery and murder. Bathsheba's son, Solomon, built the temple and finished David's dream. God loves to redeem failures and ultimately bring gold out of the fire.

Saul of Tarsus was a Pharisee's Pharisee. He orchestrated the stoning of Stephen, according to Acts 7:58, *". . . and they cast him out of the city and stoned him. And the witnesses laid down their clothes at the feet of a young man named Saul."* Saul single–handedly decimated the church at Jerusalem according to Acts 8:1, *"Now Saul was consenting to his death. At that time a great persecution arose against the church which was at Jerusalem; and they were all scattered throughout the regions of Judea and Samaria, except the apostles."* Thousands of believers were displaced because of his rage. Did God redeem it? The church at Antioch was born as a result. Acts 9:1–2 states:

Then Saul, still breathing threats and murder against the disciples of the Lord, went to the high priest and asked letters from him to the synagogues of Damascus, so that if he found any who were of the Way, whether men or women, he might bring them bound to Jerusalem.

Saul devastated the early church until a radical and dramatic conversion took place. Saul could have lived in shame all his days according to Galatians 1:13–14:

> For you have heard of my former conduct in Judaism, how I persecuted the church of God beyond measure and tried to destroy it. And I advanced in Judaism beyond many of my contemporaries in my own nation, being more exceedingly zealous for the traditions of my fathers.

Paul earnestly prayed for his kinsman, the Jewish nation, to be grafted back in and the result was a revelation of God's ultimate purpose for the church and how the Jew would be grafted back in once the "fullness of the Gentiles" had arrived. God redeemed Saul's failure and answered his heart's cry with a revelation of an end–of–the–age harvest. "Sure Mercy" is a covenant God extends to redeem our failures and make them serve His developmental purposes!

One of the great fruits of failure is compassion which rises for all those with parallel experiences. Moses' refusal to let go of God saved both the nation and his brother Aaron. When we ask about the origin of this depth of compassion, only one possibility emerges—his own experience with self–effort and the forty year price tag attached. Moses, David, and Paul were three of the greatest leaders in the Bible, all sharing a common experience. They developed a relationship with a God who was so great He could redeem their past failures and turn them into a platform for their greatest victories. The God of Moses, David and Paul has not changed. He is still extending an invitation to all who will come, promising to redeem their greatest failures and empowering them to extend His Kingdom! Please add your name to the list!

There is such freedom in this truth:
God uses failure too
Through it He forges inner fruit
With power for changing you

And He has signed and sealed it all
With legal covenant
The end result—you're guaranteed
The mercy that He's sent

Chapter 2

Possessing Confidence

The Key to the Throne Room

Ephesians 3:8–12 says:

> To me, who am less than the least of all the saints, this grace was
> given, that I should preach among the Gentiles the unsearchable
> riches of Christ, and to make all people see what is the fellow-
> ship of the mystery, which from the beginning of the ages has
> been hidden in God who created all things through Jesus Christ;
> to the intent that now the manifold wisdom of God might be
> made known by the Church to the principalities and powers in
> the heavenly places, according to the eternal purpose which He
> accomplished in Christ Jesus our Lord, in whom we have boldness
> and access with confidence through faith in Him.

The boldness to access God's presence with confidence through
faith in Him is the goal expressed in the New Testament for every
believer. The sad fact is that the majority of the church lacks this
confidence to access the Throne Room and really believe that God's

promises can be appropriated for them. The requirement to function in boldness and access with confidence through faith is the real goal and must become a reality in order for the church to fulfill what is prophesied for the last days.

The Greek word translated "confidence" has a root which *The Complete Word Study New Testament Dictionary* defines as, "to persuade another to receive a belief."[2] If it is possible to persuade believers to accept the covenant of "Sure Mercy" then they will have the confidence necessary to birth and participate in God's government. **Confidence is the fruit of a process which starts with forgiveness, transitions to justification, accepts righteousness, and appropriates redemption.** Acts 13 leads us toward this progression in verses 38–39 when it says:

> Therefore let it be known to you, brethren, that through this Man is preached to you the forgiveness of sins; and by Him everyone who believes is justified from all things from which you could not be justified by the law of Moses.

Confidence begins with accepting forgiveness of sin, bought and paid for through the sacrifice of Jesus. Without the shedding of blood, there is no remission of sin. Jesus shed His blood in five different places for the forgiveness of sin and our ability to resist the accuser of the brethren. Five is the number for grace. Every one of the five different places purchases a specific application of redemption.

Luke 22:43–44 says, *"Then an angel appeared to Him from heaven, strengthening Him. And being in agony, He prayed more earnestly. And His sweat became like great drops of blood falling down to the ground."*

---

2. *The Complete Word Study Dictionary: New Testament.* Ed. Spiros Zodhiates, Warren Baker, and George Hadjiantoniou. ©1992. AMG Publishers (Chattanooga, TN). Used by permission.

Jesus resisted the temptation to walk away from the Father's purpose for His life because of the agony and pain involved. His blood was shed to redeem every single incidence of refusing God's purpose and plan because of price. We have to accept forgiveness *because* of what Jesus did for us. His blood cleanses from disobedience.

Matthew 27:26 records the second place Jesus shed His blood and it says, *"Then he released Barabbas to them; and when he had scourged Jesus, he delivered Him to be crucified."* This scourging was for sin, sickness, and disease of all mankind— *"by His stripes we are healed."*

The very next verse gives us the third place His blood was shed. Verses 27–29 says:

> Then the soldiers of the governor took Jesus into the Praetorium and gathered the whole garrison around Him. And they stripped Him and put a scarlet robe on Him. When they had twisted a crown of thorns, they put it on His head, and a reed in His right hand. And they bowed the knee before Him and mocked Him, saying, 'Hail, King of the Jews!'

Jesus endured a crown of thorns representing ridicule, mockery, and persecution. Every person who denies the Lord by retreating in silence amidst ridicule, mockery, or persecution has a specific opportunity to redeem their spiritual cowardice. Jesus carried that crown of thorns to redeem every one of us from retreating in the face of persecution. His blood was shed for us.

In Acts 4 when the early church faced persecution, they agreed together asking for boldness, signs, and wonders, based on Psalm 2. God answered by filling them with His Spirit a second time. They obtained what they prayed for.

Luke 23:33 gives us the fourth place that Jesus shed His blood and it says, *"And when they had come to the place called Calvary, there they crucified Him, and the criminals, one on the right hand and the other on the left."* They drove the nails in His hands and He was affixed to the cross and lifted up for every aspect of failure that a human can make. Hearing it is one thing, while seeing it depicted in a movie is quite another, but *accepting* it is the ultimate goal!

The fifth and final loss of blood came when the soldier plunged the spear in His side to see if, in fact, He had already died. Isaiah 53:5 states, *"He was pierced/wounded for our transgressions, He was bruised for our iniquities; The chastisement for our peace was upon Him."* Jesus paid the price to heal every person pierced by the devastating words of family, friends and foes. Proverbs 12:18 says, *"There is one who speaks like the piercings of a sword, But the tongue of the wise promotes health."* The covenant of "Sure Mercy" goes beyond promoting to guaranteeing. Never was anyone marred like Jesus was marred, completely and totally for our **forgiveness.** But accepting forgiveness is only the first step toward confidence, because if forgiveness is not followed by accepting justification then there is still room for condemnation. Romans 3:21–26 says:

> But now the righteousness of God apart from the law is revealed, being witnessed by the Law and the Prophets, even the righteousness of God which is through faith in Jesus Christ to all and on all who believe. For there is no difference; for all have sinned and fall short of the glory of God, **being justified freely** (without paying for it) by His grace though the redemption that is in Christ Jesus, whom God set forth to be a propitiation by His blood, through faith, to demonstrate His righteousness, because in His forbearance God had passed over the sins that were previously committed.

It is one thing to accept forgiveness. It is another step to accept justification. Justification means "just as if I never did it." Justification removes the grounds for accusation and condemnation. Only when we have accepted what Jesus did through His blood to justify us and reposition us in God can we ever go on to complete the growth process necessary to possess the confidence to function governmentally.

Romans 5:15–16 state:

> But the free gift is not like the offense. For if by the one man's offense many died, much more the grace of God and the gift by the grace of the one Man, Jesus Christ, abounded to many. And the gift is not like that which came through the one who sinned. For the judgment which came from one offense resulted in condemnation, but the free gift which came from many offenses resulted in justification.

Are we willing to accept God's forgiveness and His justification? If we fail to take the "justification" step *then* we allow the enemy to hinder all progress because we cannot go on to righteousness, redemption and confidence. Accepting **justification** is essential.

Romans 5:17–19 says:

> For if by the one man's offense death reigned through the one, much more those who receive abundance of grace and of the gift of righteousness will reign in life through the One, Jesus Christ. Therefore, as through one man's offense judgment came to all men, resulting in condemnation, even so through one Man's righteous act the free gift came to all men, resulting in justification of life. For as by one man's disobedience many were made sinners, so also by one Man's obedience many will be made righteous.

The gift of **righteousness** is the next step after receiving justification. Righteousness is the realization that there is nothing between us and God to hinder communication or relationship. It is the gift of righteousness which imparts the boldness to go into the Throne Room. It is the gift of righteousness that leads us toward confidence. If we don't have the time to fully explore the gift of righteousness, then we stop the maturing process. Accepting righteousness is essential in progressing toward the confidence that Jesus bought and paid for!

Redemption is the next step. Redemption is really the fruit of accepting the covenant of "Sure Mercy." Redemption is when God takes our failure and turns it into the platform for our ministry, or the success of attaining His purpose. Isaiah 55:1–3 issues an open invitation to the world to accept God's covenant of "Sure Mercy":

> Ho! Everyone who thirsts, Come to the waters; And you who have no money, Come, buy and eat. Yes, come buy wine and milk Without money and without price. Why do you spend money for what is not bread? And your wages for what does not satisfy? Listen diligently to Me, and eat what is good, And let your soul delight itself in abundance. Incline your ear, and come to Me. Hear, and your soul shall live; And I will make an **everlasting covenant** with you—**the Sure Mercies of David.**

If we are hungry we can have the covenant of "Sure Mercy." The real question is, What is this covenant of "Sure Mercy" and how do we discover what all it entails? The covenant of "Sure Mercy" was delivered by the prophet Nathan to David in Second Samuel 7:1–3:

> Now it came to pass when the king was dwelling in his house, and the LORD had given him rest from all his enemies all around, that the king said to Nathan the prophet, "See now, I dwell in a house of cedar, but the ark of God dwells inside tent curtains." Then Nathan said to the king, "Go, do all that is in your heart, for the LORD is with you."

David had it in his heart to build God a house. In the process of building his own house in Jerusalem, after a significant number of victories and a tremendous amount of wealth from the spoil of the nations, his heart convicted him of building his own house ahead of God's. This may be one of life's greatest pitfalls. Spending all our effort on ourselves without considering leaving a legacy for impacting future generations has dramatic eternal repercussions. Nathan's initial response to David's inquiry was, *"Go do all that is in your heart, for the L*ORD* is with you."* Later that night, God came to modify that prophetic word and Nathan had to return again to outline what God was saying. Second Samuel 7:4–7 states:

> But it happened that night that the word of the LORD came to Nathan, saying, "Go and tell My servant David, 'Thus says the LORD: "Would you build a house for Me to dwell in? For I have not dwelt in a house since the time that I brought the children of Israel up from Egypt, even to this day, but have moved about in a tent and in a tabernacle. In all the places where I have walked with all the children of Israel, have I ever spoken a word to anyone from the tribes of Israel, whom I commanded to shepherd My people Israel, saying, 'Why have you not built Me a house of cedar?'"'

God is asking David if He has ever, from the days of Moses until then, asked anybody about building a permanent house. God wanted so much to be *with* the people wherever they went, that a permanent house was never considered. And God brings this point, for obvious underlying reasons, before David. He goes on to say in verses 11b–16 that He will build David a house and give him an everlasting covenant.

> Also the LORD tells you that He will make you a house. When your days are fulfilled and you rest with your fathers, I will set

up your seed after you, who will come from your body, and I
will establish his kingdom. He shall build a house for My name
and I will establish the throne of his kingdom forever. I will be
his Father, and he shall be My son. If he commits iniquity, I will
chasten him with the rod of men and with the blows of the sons
of men. But My mercy shall not depart from him, as I took it
from Saul, whom I removed from before you. And your house
and your kingdom shall be established forever before you. Your
throne shall be established forever.

The key verse establishing the covenant of "Sure Mercy" is verse 15
which says, *"But My mercy shall not depart from him, **as I took it from
Saul**, whom I removed from before you."* If we want to know what
the essence of the covenant of "Sure Mercy" is, all we have to do is
return to the point where God removes Saul. That event transpired
in First Samuel 15. Verses 1–3 say:

Samuel also said to Saul, "The LORD sent me to anoint you king
over His people, over Israel. Now therefore, heed the voice of the
words of the LORD. Thus says the LORD of hosts; 'I will punish
what Amalek did to Israel, how he laid wait for him on the way
when he came up from Egypt. Now go and attack Amalek, and
utterly destroy all that they have, and do not spare them. But kill
both man and woman, infant and nursing child, ox and sheep,
camel and donkey.'"

The God of war assigns Saul to go to war with Amalek. He orders
every single man, woman, child and animal to be killed. Secretly
I questioned the righteousness of this "kill them all" strategy for
many years. I couldn't imagine a culture so perverse and demonized
as to warrant such an order, until I saw Muslim children and their

parents dancing with glee at the destruction of the Twin Towers on 9/11. Now I can relate to the order God gave Saul. I can agree with God's removal of Saul for not killing them all. God **knew** what needed to be done! This is the God of the Bible. This is the God who is the same, yesterday, today and forever. If this Jesus sounds strange, it is because the popular social gospel of the last fifty years has purposefully neglected Jesus the Judge in an attempt to gain followers. The God of the Old Covenant has not changed. This is the same God who, in Revelation, orders the annihilation of a third of mankind because of their rebellion. When ministers choose to present only covenant blessing for fear of losing people, the fruit of their ministry turns the God of the Bible into a "Sugar Daddy" who does whatever we want Him to do when we want Him to do it. Some seeker–sensitive ministers have recast God into man's image! Coming out of a church culture can be paramount when God has been presented as made in our image. Such a culture sounds like this: "Jesus will meet your need." God is presented as one who so loves everyone He panders to personal need. The righteous God who commands repentance is remade into a sloppy agape dispenser of blessing. This underlying message is the primary theme presented by many. Is it any wonder there is no fear of God in many of our politicians, because long ago the fear of God left many pulpits. In verses 7–9 of First Samuel 15, we continue to see the progression of Saul's rebellion against God's Word. It says:

> And Saul attacked the Amalekites, from Havilah all the way to Shur, which is east of Egypt. He also took Agag king of the Amalekites alive, and utterly destroyed all the people with the edge of the sword. But Saul and the people spared Agag and the best of the sheep, the oxen, the fatlings, the lambs, and all that was good, and were unwilling to utterly destroy them. But everything despised and worthless, that they utterly destroyed.

Saul and the people spared Agag and the best of the animals and everything that they had use for they kept and were utterly unwilling to destroy it. It was for the refusal to wage war in God's way—total annihilation—that Saul lost His kingship! God never asked anyone to fight an antiseptic war. When any nation loses the will to fight God's way, they might as well surrender. The American will for war slipped away during Vietnam! None of this milk–toast and mush theology existed in our nation during World War II. In the 1940s when we sent our military to war, we sent them to annihilate the enemy. If this mindset had not existed, the atomic bombs would never have been dropped and thousands of lives would have been lost on both sides in the taking of Japan. The consequences of rejecting the biblical mindset for war in Scripture was the prompt loss of leadership! Any Japanese soldier fighting from his Buddhist temple would have died in the destruction of the temple. Anyone suggesting the military not destroy a mosque from which the enemy was firing would have been ridiculed in World War II. Oh, that it were the same today! If we don't *think* straight then we can't *act* straight! Because our forefathers in previous generations thought straight, having their minds renewed to Scripture, then whenever they went to war they didn't go in a "politically correct" way. They went the Bible way. They went God's way! By going to war God's way, according to Romans 13:4, they executed wrath on evildoers and they spared many lives.

The deception that is upon Islamic terrorists is so deep that they take innocent peoples' heads off, thinking they are doing God service. As abominable as that deception is, it is no worse than the deception gripping any person or political party that thinks we can go to war in a "politically correct" way, or that we can reason with radical Muslims and diffuse their anger. There is no difference between those two levels of **deception.** They are the same. One *produces* murder and mayhem and the other *encourages* it! Neville Chamberlain, as the prime minister of Great Britain in 1940, was of such a spirit. His policies encouraged Hitler. The same people who spit on us as we returned from Vietnam are polluting the minds of college kids, populating political parties possessed by pacifism, promoting homosexuality, and pursuing the murder of innocent children through abortion. Yet they can't understand why we face increasing national adversity! The spirit of pacifism is alive and well, growing in our culture, and is so far removed from biblical thinking as to constitute an abomination that may ultimately cost us our nation!

Saul lost his kingship for not killing everyone! When God goes to war He annihilates the enemy and there is no apology to any sector of society that spawned the perpetrators. The prophet Samuel confronts Saul and in First Samuel 15:22–23 we see the first of three major losses for Saul:

> Then Samuel said: 'Has the LORD as great delight in burnt offerings and sacrifices, As in obeying the voice of the LORD? Behold, to obey is better than sacrifice, And to heed than the fat of rams. For rebellion is as the sin of witchcraft, And stubbornness is as iniquity and idolatry. Because you have rejected the word of the LORD, He also has rejected you from being king.'

Saul lost his office of being king. Any politician who leads a nation to war should go to win. He should willingly and utterly release the military to annihilate the enemy. Harry Truman was successful in ending World War II but reigned in the military in Korea, subjecting millions of Chinese to the torture of Communism. Truman fired General MacArthur, but history has proven MacArthur right! MacArthur wanted to finish the war God's way. After my experience in Vietnam, I felt so strongly about this issue that as the first Iraq war approached, I was compelled to write a letter to the first President Bush concerning his choice of how to conduct the war. It was read on the House floor and appears in the *Congressional Record.*

February 15, 1991

The Honorable George Herbert Walker Bush
President of the United States
The White House
Washington, D.C. 20500

Dear Mr President:

I am writing to thank you primarily, and secondarily the Congress, for taking a stand that is bringing healing to the hearts of this and many other wounded Vietnam Veterans.

The greatest wounds of Vietnam were not inflicted in the rice paddies of Southeast Asia, but were scars seared in our hearts from our own government who sent us off to war but refused to let us win. Every soldier knew the military could have won the Vietnam war in six months if our elected leaders would have only turned us loose. Going to war and coming home with a victory is something to be proud of, but facing death and coming home with nothing is a shame.

For nearly two decades, I have felt the Vietnam years of my life were a worthless waste until you stood before this nation and declared, "We will not fight this war, with one arm tied behind us." The three times I have seen you make that statement on television have healed my heart by redeeming my Vietnam experience.

For the first time, value and worth have risen from the ashes of what twenty years ago seemed like a fiery furnace. The value of Vietnam I saw demonstrated through your lips, and approved by the Congress was: a generation of political leaders **learned how not** to conduct a war. My experience now has great value because the President of the United States and a majority of Congress learned something through it and are conducting Foreign Policy accordingly.

Those of us who experienced Vietnam have lived with the truth of Proverbs 18:14, "The spirit of a man will sustain him in sickness, but who can bear a broken spirit." All one hundred and sixty-one combat missions I flew as a Navy Reconnaissance pilot are now much more than entries in a log book. Thank you, Mr. President, for helping heal this wounded warrior!

Respectfully yours,
Al Houghton

All leaders who send us off to war and refuse to allow the military to win should promptly lose their office. Saul lost his office! The second loss is outlined in verses 24–26:

> Then Saul said to Samuel, "I have sinned, for I have transgressed the commandment of the Lord and your words, because I feared the people and obeyed their voice. Now therefore, please pardon my sin, and return with me, that I may worship the Lord." But Samuel said to Saul, "I will not return with you, for you have rejected the word of the Lord, and the Lord has rejected you from being king over Israel."

Although the language is nearly identical, verse 23b and verse 26b have two words that distinguish them. Verse 23b says, *"He also has* *rejected you from **being king**."* Verse 26b says, *". . . and the* LORD *has rejected you from being king **over Israel**."* The addition of the words *"over Israel"* indicate the second thing Saul lost was his call. Losing the office and losing the call are very different things. If you lose your office but don't lose your call, you can get back in office again. That happened to David when Absalom took his throne. The covenant of "Sure Mercy" guaranteed David would regain his office. Once Saul lost his call, there could be no restoration. Saul lost his office, he lost his call, and the third thing he lost is outlined in chapter 16, verse 14. It says, *"But the Spirit of the* LORD *departed from Saul, and a distressing spirit from the* LORD *troubled him."*

Saul lost three things. First, he lost his office, second, he lost his call, and third, he lost the anointing of the Holy Spirit to walk in the office and fulfill the call. Now the picture of the covenant of "Sure Mercy" can move toward completion, because God's promise of mercy to David and his seed had a specific purpose. The purpose of **"Sure Mercy"** is in guaranteeing contributions toward Kingdom growth even when personal moral failure occurs. The covenant of "Sure Mercy" guarantees establishing our contributions. Personal failure will not cost us our call. We do not have to lose the anointing of the Holy Spirit to walk in the office and fulfill the call. God gave David an awesome covenant. But the question we have to ask is, Why? What is so important about an individual contribution that God would offer to redeem our failures so we can regain our office (after repentance), keep our call, and possess the anointing to finish the race? The answer is in the passage.

Second Samuel 7:12–13 states:

> When your days are fulfilled and you rest with your fathers, I will set up your seed after you, who will come from your body, and I will establish his kingdom. He shall build a house for My name, and I will establish the throne of his kingdom forever.

If David did not have the covenant of "Sure Mercy" then God would have had to start over whenever there was disqualifying failure of any of His leaders. He went on to say to David in verse 16, *"And your house and your kingdom shall be established forever before you. Your throne shall be established forever."* The covenant of "Sure Mercy" allows God to establish the work of our hands in contribution to the building of His Kingdom without the loss of that work when we commit a failure that deserves judgment. The covenant of "Sure Mercy" is perhaps one of the most awesome things that God ever offered man.

Not only did Isaiah extend the covenant of "Sure Mercy" to the world, but Paul quotes it in Acts 13. In the longest recorded message of the apostle Paul's ministry, we find the covenant of "Sure Mercy" at the core! Acts 13:32–34 says:

> And we declare to you glad tidings—that promise which was made to the fathers. God has fulfilled this for us, their children, in that He has raised up Jesus. As it is also written in the second Psalm: "You are My Son, Today I have begotten You." And that He raised Him from the dead, no more to return to corruption, He has spoken thus: "I will give you the sure mercies of David."

This revelation which he brought to the church at Antioch was what Jesus bought and paid for in extending the covenant of "Sure Mercy." In Christ Jesus there is "Sure Mercy"—the same "Sure Mercy" that He gave to David; the same "Sure Mercy" that allows Him to establish the work of our hands; the same "Sure Mercy" that says if you have a failure, you don't have to lose your office, you don't have to lose your call, and you don't have to lose the anointing of the Holy Spirit to walk in the office and fulfill the call.

The covenant of "Sure Mercy" not only deals with our failures and helps us accept forgiveness, justification, and righteousness, but it is in fact the key to redemption. It is the covenant of "Sure Mercy" that guarantees the redemption of that failure so that it will ultimately praise God and bring growth to His Kingdom. It is time to pursue one of the finest applications of the revelation of redemption that God ever offered to man—**the covenant of "Sure Mercy."**

Just as God gave to David
He offers it to you
The mercy-sure to run your race
And redeem failure too

Chapter 3

Redeeming Failure

Isaiah ministered from about 740 to 680 B.C. That is nearly sixty years. In chapter 45:1–4, Isaiah prophesied about a king who would be born a hundred plus years before it happened. From the succeeding verses in this passage we gain some of the attributes of God. He says in verses 5–8:

> I am the LORD, and there is no other; There is no God besides Me. I will gird you, though you have not known Me, That they may know from the rising of the sun to its setting That there is none beside Me. I am the LORD, and there is no other; I form the light and create the darkness, I make peace and create calamity; I, the LORD, do all these things. Rain down, you heavens, from above, And let the skies pour down righteousness; Let the earth open, let them bring forth salvation, And let righteousness spring up together, I, the LORD have created it.

God has tremendous foreknowledge and His omnipotence is something we rely on. In His foreknowledge He can look ahead and see the choices we will make before we ever get there. This is alluded to in Acts 4:27–28 which says:

> For truly against Your holy Servant Jesus, whom You anointed, both Herod and Pontius Pilate, with the Gentiles and the people of Israel, were gathered together to do whatever Your hand and Your purpose determined before to be done.

God is a God of foreknowledge. He sees and knows the choices we are going to make before we make them. He doesn't stop us from making them. The price of being made in the image and likeness of God is being accountable for our actions as creators. When we create evil, we reap evil. The reason we avoid sin is so we don't have to live the remainder of our lives under the penalty of those actions! Any laws which lessen the penalty encourage the sin!

The year was 1998. I was in Stuttgart, Germany, ministering and the Lord spoke this to me. "When did I speak to My servant David about his son Solomon, before or after he met Bathsheba?" I said, "I don't know." God said, "Find out."

In Second Samuel 11 David met Bathsheba in verses 1–3:

> Now it came to pass in the spring of the year, at the time when kings go out to battle, that David sent Joab and his servants with him, and all Israel, and they destroyed the people of Ammon and besieged Rabbah. But David remained at Jerusalem. Then it happened one evening that David arose from his bed and walked on the roof of the king's house. And from the roof he saw a woman bathing, and the woman was very beautiful to behold. So David sent and inquired about the woman. And someone said, 'Is this not Bathsheba, the daughter of Eliam, the wife of Uriah the Hittite?'

Four chapters before, in Second Samuel 7 God gave David the covenant of "Sure Mercy," enabling him to establish all the work of his hands. The answer to the Lord's question was, four chapters *before* David met Bathsheba, God gave him a covenant of "Sure Mercy." The implications of that, considering God's foreknowledge, are spectacular. Before David ever reached the pinnacle failure of his life, God already looked ahead, saw it and redeemed it. We say to ourselves, "How can that be?" In Second Samuel 12, David is confronted with his sin by the prophet Nathan, the same one who gave him the covenant of Sure Mercy. David repented. We go on to see in verses 24–25 the child of adultery dies under penalty of sin. The second becomes a child of covenant mercy. Verse 24 says, "... *And the* LORD *loved him.*" I'm sure God tweaked every Pharisee in Israel by bringing Solomon out of a relationship that started in adultery and murder. The wisest man who ever lived, who had the greatest anointing for wisdom ever to fall upon man, came from a relationship that started in adultery and murder. How could God do that?

With the covenant of "Sure Mercy," God did not have to find another David and start over. He covenanted to redeem his failure. Redemption means you buy back part of the penalty and bring good out of the evil. Redemption allows us to live and finish our call! All sin has repercussions which cost. David lived the rest of his life with those consequences. God redeemed his contribution to the Kingdom. You buy it back. You turn it from a negative to a positive. God brought the very one who would fulfill David's heart in building God a house out of a relationship He had to redeem! Jesus bought and paid for the covenant of "Sure Mercy" and He extends it to us. Surely we can extend it to each other and surely we will appropriate it and say "yes" to God and let Him redeem our greatest failures. We still have to live with the fruit of sin. Living with the fruit of sin is a great deterrent to not committing it! The loss of Absalom, Amnon, Ahithophel, and others was very painful. David lived the rest of his life with the fruit of his sin. Redemption enabled David's vision to be fulfilled from the fruit of his greatest failure.

The progression of accepting **forgiveness**, accepting **justification**, accepting the gift of **righteousness** and accepting **redemption** is only complete when we let God turn the failure into the platform for our greatest fulfillment. That is redemption in action. What lies in our background no longer need remain hidden. We must bring it to God and allow Him to redeem. He is the Redeemer. He wants to redeem. We cannot become an agent of redemption until we have allowed Him to redeem our failures. It is a process that God takes us through. It is time to walk this process to conclusion so we can make the Kingdom contribution that God ordained.

Redemption in action
Turns failure to gold
And the fruit of redemption
Is sweet to behold

Chapter 4

Eight Steps of Restoration

Second Samuel 12:13–14 records steps one and two:

> Then David said to Nathan, "I have sinned against the LORD."
> And Nathan said to David, "The LORD also has put away your
> sin; you shall not die. However, because by this deed you have
> given great occasion to the enemies of the LORD to blaspheme,
> the child also who is born to you shall surely die."

In step one, David acknowledges his sin. Restoration can never occur
if the perpetrating party refuses to open the primary passageway.
Acknowledging or "owning our stuff" is an act of transparency and
humility which God requires. A failure to acknowledge ends all
hope of restoration. If there is not full disclosure and acceptance of
responsibility by the offender, save yourself the heartache of attempting to restore one who balks at completing phase one. In step two
the offending party accepts the righteous judgment and restoration
plan as outlined by those to whom he has submitted. Step two is
every bit as necessary in determining future success in a restoration
plan. Do not proceed if there is hesitation at either stage one or two.

Submission at the first two levels yields a very high success rate while failure in either one usually dooms the process.

Verse 20 outlines the key elements of the restoration process: *"So David arose from the ground, washed and anointed himself, and changed his clothes; and he went into the house of the Lord and worshiped. Then he went to his own house; and when he requested, they set food before him, and he ate."* Step three demands a personal choice to arise in the midst of failure. Every person must choose to get up and transition from the position of mourning over their failure to accepting God's forgiveness. This means accepting what Jesus bought with His blood. David had to choose to get up. No one could pick him up. This is something that has to register in the heart. We must help people through the devastation of what their sin has produced with an attitude reflecting grace and forgiveness. Many choose to live in the paralysis of the past. The apostle Paul tells us in Philippians that *"forgetting the things that are behind we choose to press on toward the upper call of God in Christ Jesus."* Oftentimes we have to reach out to those in failure with that attitude. It is time to see God arise over His people and to be agents of restoration. This is the function of mercy. It has a most practical application. We become the hands, heart and words of God extended to those in failure, enabling them to arise.

Step number four is also in verse 20 of chapter twelve. David makes the choice to wash. Washing is the process necessary to cleanse the conscience, enabling the individual to pick up God's call. The conscience has to be washed of all the effects of the sin. Each of us have to accept the fact that righteousness is something that is God–given but relationally nurtured. It is not something we earn. It is a gift that must be taken. Washing is absolutely essential to restore this reality. Washing cleanses self–condemnation. David washes the shame away, which is necessary in moving toward restored confidence in his gifting and calling.

The fifth step recorded in verse 20 is the choice to anoint himself. This reflects the anointing of being clean. He is returning with confidence to ministry. There are two different Hebrew words for "anointing." One is the anointing that is a one–time event which comes when a person is initiated into ministry. David answered the call when Samuel poured the anointing oil over his head. The anointing that David is experiencing here is not an application of the holy anointing oil. This anointing reflects the joy of being made clean and the restoration of confidence attained through God's forgiveness. It is a very important step in transformation. It is the fruit of restoration. Oftentimes people need our support in order to accomplish this washing. It is through corporate acceptance, confirmation and encouragement of the church that this spiritual washing is completed. Approval must be shown and accepted to continue.

The sixth step David takes in verse 20 is the changing of his clothes. This signifies putting on the kingly robes of divine authority that are appropriate to the position of the believer. This is a step that is essential because it becomes a statement in the realm of the spirit. This act declares we have returned to the authority of our gifting and calling. We cannot do this if we are not clean or if we have not appropriated a restored sense of righteousness. A restored sense of acceptance by the body is foundational for this stage. This is where the body is very necessary in completing and restoring God's purpose for the individual. David put on his kingly robes so he could once again stand in the office and fulfill the call. The same thing has to be done in the realm of the spirit for every individual who has walked through failure.

In step seven, David returns to the house of the LORD, worships, and reconnects with God. The sin is over. The restoration is nearly complete. He can't change the past. He knows it. It is time to reconnect with the LORD and receive the boldness that comes because his sin is cleansed. David is ready. He embraces God in worship. This is the seventh step in moving back toward full restoration. Are we willing to extend this to those who fail and to those who hurt us in the process? God has revealed His heart in redemption. Now it must become our heart.

In step number eight, David has to become an agent of restoration. There is a natural tendency to distance ourselves from all involved in embarrassing failures. David could have easily done that. Instead David had to extend the same mercy to Bathsheba that God extended to him. In the process of that extension he becomes God's heart and God's hands of mercy. What would happen if the church began to move in restoration? How would our communities react to such demonstrations? Perhaps we would gain a reputation of doing what we preach. How would the world react if the church were actually to become the agent of restoration for the failures of our society? In Isaiah 55 we are promised what God will do if we extend His covenant of "Sure Mercy." Verses 3–5 declare, concerning David:

> Incline your ear, and come to Me. Hear, and your soul shall live; And I will make an everlasting covenant with you—the sure mercies of David. Indeed I have given him as a witness to the people, A leader and commander for the people. Surely you shall call a nation you do not know, And nations who do not know you shall run to you, Because of the LORD your God, And the Holy One of Israel; For He has glorified you.

God promises that we shall call a nation we do not know, and nations who do not know us shall run to us, once they see the manifestation of mercy in our lives. Apparently the world is waiting to see this covenant of mercy in operation. If we can manifest it, we qualify for an anointing that will cause nations to run to us. How are we doing? It is much easier to judge than to extend mercy. We can judge leaders, throw them out, put them on the sideline, banish them from all leadership, never to be seen or heard again. The problem with that path is that it disqualifies us for the anointing which wins nations. Shouldn't we consider changing our ways? When our friends fail, they become our greatest opportunity to access new spiritual realms. We have to walk them through each of the eight steps. If we embrace the process, then we can take the promise in our mouth and God will honor it.

In Isaiah 55:6–9 we're encouraged to do that very thing:

> Seek the LORD while He may be found, Call upon Him while He is near. Let the wicked forsake his way, And the unrighteous man his thoughts; Let him return to the LORD And He will have mercy on him; And to our God, For He will abundantly pardon. "For My thoughts are not your thoughts, Nor are your ways My ways," says the LORD. "For as the heavens are higher than the earth, So are My ways higher than your ways, And My thoughts than your thoughts."

The promise is that when the individual returns to the Lord, God will have mercy on him and He will abundantly pardon—not sparsely pardon—but abundantly pardon! Abundant pardon has to have a demonstration from people. We have to supply the words and the hands of abundance. The touch of God has to come through the corporate church. God will not allow us to extend it to the nation unless we consistently faithfully extend it to each other. Nations desperately need the mercy of God. How do we qualify to extend it to a nation? We first have to extend it to each other in our natural and spiritual families.

Verses 10–13 of the same passage says:

> For as the rain comes down, and the snow from heaven, And do not return there, But water the earth, And make it bring forth and

bud, That it may give seed to the sower And bread to the eater, So shall My word be that goes forth from My mouth; It shall not return to Me void, But it shall accomplish what I please, And it shall prosper in the thing for which I send it. For you shall go out with joy, And be led out with peace; The mountains and the hills Shall break forth into singing before you, And all the trees of the field shall clap their hands. Instead of the thorn shall come up the cypress tree, And instead of the brier shall come up the myrtle tree; And it shall be to the LORD for a name, For an everlasting sign that shall not be cut off.

Thorns and briers were always signs of unproductive land due to sin generating curses. When God created the earth and gave regional territory to people groups, they could forfeit their right to the land by filling it with iniquity. In Leviticus 22 God warned the Israelites not to adopt statutes of the nations they dispossessed because the land would vomit them out. When they filled it with iniquity, they could no longer protect it. The four things cited in that chapter filling a land with iniquity are:

1. The sacrifice of innocent blood
2. Proliferation of witchcraft and new age
3. Rebellion as is found in the drug culture
4. Protection and promotion of homosexuality and lesbianism.

When a nation begins to reap the fruit of disobedience, the believers have an obligation to walk in the covenant of **"Sure Mercy"** and stop the judgment until a harvest can be gained. The same land that cries for a cleansing as it fills with iniquity can also rejoice when the church practices the covenant of **"Sure Mercy."** The mountains and the hills of Isaiah 55 can groan under the weight of a perverse culture, demanding judgment, or they *"break forth into singing"* when the church qualifies to proclaim the covenant of **"Sure Mercy."**

The only way we qualify to take the covenant of "Sure Mercy" and put it in our mouth is when we practice extending it to each other. God said He ordained this covenant to be spoken to a nation. We can confess it over our country when we're in prayer in the Throne Room. God says when we do, "It shall not return to Him void, but it shall accomplish what He pleases, and it shall prosper in the thing for which He sent it." When is the last time we confessed the covenant of "Sure Mercy" over our city, over our state, or over our nation? That is the call. A nation in judgment needs a people who can extend the covenant of "Sure Mercy," forestalling the judgment and gaining a harvest. God will hold the church accountable for the condition of the land in the days ahead. It's time we grew up to be agents of restoration, gaining the maximum harvest. If we pay the price, God will honor our words!

Would you extend mercy
Over your nation
Declaring redemption
Freedom and salvation?

Then move forth in mercy
Toward brother and friend
And watch the great harvest
Spring forth and extend

Chapter 5

Embracing Our Eternal Purpose

The covenant of "Sure Mercy" guarantees the continued anointing to fulfill our ordained purposes through the process of redemption and restoration. Ephesians 2:8–10 suggests that every one of us have a considerable contribution to make:

> For by grace you have been saved through faith, and that not of yourselves; it is the gift of God, not of works, lest anyone should boast. For we are His workmanship, created in Christ Jesus for good works, **which God prepared beforehand** that we should walk in them.

The picture given here is that *before* we were ever created God knew, ordained and discerned a purpose for us to fulfill. That purpose would make a significant contribution to His Kingdom. We have the free will to refuse or accept God and His purposes. To be sidelined with no hope of ever fulfilling that eternal purpose is a gross insult to the blood of Jesus. Jesus not only died for the lost, but the broken, the wounded, and the castaway! Choose this day to be broken, wounded, and castaway **no longer**! Choose to believe this covenant word.

Second Timothy 1:7–9 amplifies this truth:

> For God has not given us a spirit of fear, but of power and of love and of a sound mind. Therefore do not be ashamed of the testimony of our Lord, nor of me His prisoner, but share with me in the sufferings for the gospel according to the power of God, who has saved us and called us with a holy calling, not according to our works, but according to His own purpose and grace which was given to us in Christ Jesus before time began. . . .

In this passage, if we start at the end of the progression and work backwards, it is easier to understand. God assigns a **purpose** to each of our lives, but that purpose is specifically sovereignly chosen by Him. It is *not* according to our **ability**. Peter and Paul are perfect examples. Peter was sent to the Jews who loved pedigree. They were impressed by education and awed by a polished articulate presentation. Peter was a rough–and–tumble rugged fisherman. As a match for his audience, Peter was a double zero! The Gentiles, on the other hand, did not prize education or polish, and were sent Paul, a man of intellectual prowess and polish. It seems like God should have reversed it. He assigns purposes based on His sovereign will and it appears those purposes when passed on as assignments preclude relying on natural gifts or ability given. Paul had to use his faith to relate and communicate with the Gentiles. Peter had to use his faith to relate to the Jews. They were sent **not** according to their ability. Both men were dependent on God to help them relate. Their assignments forced them to walk in the Spirit having no confidence in the flesh.

The next thing we realize about this process is that each purpose also demands a parallel level of power to accomplish. Different purposes demand different levels of power. God is the source of all the different levels of power. He does not assign us a purpose demanding a level of power that He will not prepare us adequately to possess and administrate. The chief qualifier has never been our ability or our level of education. It has always been our **willingness to obey** the Holy Spirit and come under His direction and leadership. Each purpose demands a corresponding level of power. Matching each purpose with its corresponding level of power also requires an appropriate measure of suffering that is determined by the purpose and level of power necessary to bring it to pass.

This preparational process is defined by the baptism and the cup. Jesus experienced both the baptism and the cup. When James and John asked if they could sit one on the right hand and the other on the left in His glory, His initial response was not "no." The first question He raised for them was, "Are you willing to undergo the cup and the baptism with which I must be baptized?" Every major purpose not only has a power necessary to bring it to pass, but it has a preparational price tag that falls in two realms. Mark 10:38 highlights this principle. It says, *"But Jesus said to them, 'You do not know what you ask. Can you drink the cup that I drink, and be baptized with the baptism that I am baptized with?'"* Without flinching, without hesitation, without understanding what they were signing up for, they both said they could. Jesus' declaration, at that point, was that they would! James was martyred (beheaded) by Herod. John was exiled to Patmos and boiled in oil but supernaturally delivered. One day, when face to face with Jesus, we can ask why, within the same family, does God intervene for one and not the other?

Drinking the cup and enduring the baptism speak of two different realms of adversity. The "cup" is internal, and the most painful of all. When Jesus was on the cross His outcry was, *"My God, My God why have You forsaken Me?"* The betrayal and inactivity of the Father was the greatest degree of suffering that Jesus faced and it was very much a part of the preparational process of birthing salvation for mankind. Many of us have walked with situations, circumstances, losses and devastation for decades, which covenant promises address. Where is God and why has He fulfilled His Word for others while seemingly abandoning us? If you can relate, you know the flavor of the cup. No one need tell you how it tastes.

The issue of baptism came in enduring what the enemy could do to the body—the piercing, the stripes, the crown of thorns, the mockery and all the persecution. What Jesus endured in His body was secondary to the betrayal of the Father. The covenant of "Sure Mercy" gives us the authority to stand our ground and finish the race even when the baptism and the cup progress toward fullness. No sane person wants suffering. When suffering finds you and refuses to leave at the name of Jesus, though you persistently resist with great faith, then the baptism and cup are upon you. The only Christians capable of understanding are the ones who have tasted at parallel levels. Volumes could be written about these levels, but few have ears to hear. The baptism and the cup are mysterious!

The covenant of "Sure Mercy" in Isaiah 55 gives us a platform to claim the promise of Isaiah 54:17 which says:

"No weapon formed against you shall prosper, And every tongue which rises against you in judgment You shall condemn. This is the heritage of the servants of the LORD, And their righteousness is from Me," says the LORD.

This is a verse we have to use, proclaim, lay hold of and make part of our understanding. Once we have received forgiveness, justification, and righteousness, then the faith to walk in redemption demands maintaining an unsoiled heart. Jesus shed His blood so we could walk guiltless before Him and have the full measure of faith to trust Him to bring His purpose to pass in ministry. While the Old Testament is very clear about David's sin with Bathsheba and the murder of Uriah the Hittite, when it comes to the New Testament, there is silence. The New Testament records no mention of David's sin! It is silent because God redeemed David's failure. Will we walk the same path David did and possess the same promises? God offers but we must choose to accept! The New Testament proclaims David's victory, his fulfilling of God's ultimate purpose for his life, and the establishing of the Kingdom that became his contribution. David's life is applauded. Our life need be no different. We are even told that we need to duplicate his heart because *"he is a man after God's own heart."* The context of being a man of God's own heart deals with a "military mind set." Saul refused to execute the enemy while David volunteered. Are we willing to move God's hand militarily? Even in moral failure, David was victorious. God redeemed David's failure enabling him to complete his assignment. Are our failures any different? God will redeem ours as He did David's. Completing our God–given assignments builds the Kingdom.

Are you after God's own heart
Stirred as a "David" too
Let no failure hold you back
From what God has for you

His "Sure Mercy" guarantees
The kind of restoration
That can be the platform for
Your ministry's foundation

Chapter 6

How Should We Treat Failures?

One of the things the covenant of "Sure Mercy" addresses within the church is the issue of how we treat people in failure. Imagine realizing when Moses was forty that he would deliver the nation from Egyptian bondage. As an Israelite, locked in captivity in Egypt during those three and a half centuries, waiting for the promise of deliverance to be manifested, how would we have treated Moses in his failure? If we had known his potential, how would we have treated him?

Acts 7:24–28 says:

> And seeing one of them suffer wrong, he [Moses] defended and avenged him who was oppressed, and struck down the Egyptian. For he supposed that his brethren would have understood that God would deliver them by his hand, but they did not understand. And the next day he appeared to two of them as they were fighting, and tried to reconcile them, saying, "Men, you are brethren; why do you wrong one another?" But he who did his neighbor wrong pushed him away, saying, "Who made you a ruler and a judge over us? Do you want to kill me as you did the Egyptian yesterday?"

It seems that the church, like Israel, has a knack through both attitude and action of "pushing away" those who have failures, as Moses was pushed away. Through judgment, we kill our wounded or push them into fleeing for another forty years! If we could have discerned God's will, purpose, plan and anointing for Moses when he was forty, would we have pushed him away? Can we afford to prolong God's preparational process through criticism and judgment? This brings the issue to the forefront of how we are treating people whose failures God desires to redeem. Are we destroying with our words the major deliverance for which we pray? Future opportunities to witness God's glory often come in the form of people in failure. How we respond determines what we get from the Lord.

Second Samuel 16:5–8 records David's flight from Jerusalem when Absalom assumes the throne:

> Now when King David came to Bahurim, there was a man from the family of the house of Saul, whose name was Shimei the son of Gera, coming from there. He came out, cursing continuously as he came. And he threw stones at David and at all the servants of King David. And all the people and all the mighty men were on his right hand and on his left. Also Shimei said thus when he cursed: "Come out! Come out! You bloodthirsty man, you rogue! The LORD has brought upon you all the blood of the house of Saul, in whose place you have reigned, and the LORD has delivered the kingdom into the hand of Absalom your son. So now you are caught in your own evil, because you are a bloodthirsty man!"

Shimei cursed David as he went, accusing him along the way. The question is, what would Shimei have done differently if he could have discerned and known that God would take David's greatest failure, redeem it, and make him an example to all Israel of God's covenant of "Sure Mercy"? God redeemed David's failure in a variety of ways, one of which was a completely transformed heart which extended mercy throughout the remainder of his life! He made it possible to build a temple of mercy that blessed the nation for many years.

If Shimei could have seen the latter part of David's life, I rather suspect his attitude and judgment would have been entirely different. But this raises an issue for us. How many people have we viewed through their failure rather than their future and consequently condemned, skewered, devastated, criticized or incarcerated with our words? Looking through the lens of the covenant of mercy changes the view! Can we change the way we view people in failure? If we don't, we'll probably never gain the full measure of what Isaiah promised.

When we take the covenant of "Sure Mercy" and put it in our mouth, when we speak it, when we declare it, when we run toward failures to restore them instead of running away and condemning, then we will see God's glory. Serving mercy enables receiving mercy for our own failures! *Then* and only then can we put the word in our mouth and begin to demonstrate it. For those who have failures in our midst, God says, "I will restore you so that having received mercy you qualify to extend mercy over cities and over nations." Isaiah declares in 55:12–13:

> For you shall go out with joy, And be led out with peace; The mountains and the hills Shall break forth unto singing before you, And all the trees of the field shall clap their hands. Instead of the thorn shall come up the cypress tree, And instead of the brier shall come up the myrtle tree; And it shall be to the LORD for a name For an everlasting sign that shall not be cut off.

The thorns and the briers are examples of curses that come upon the land for sin. The land needs to be redeemed. It is the covenant of "Sure Mercy" in the mouth of God's people proclaimed over regions that can stop the judgment and bring forth a season of salvation. But the qualifier is simple. Number one, we have to appropriate it for ourselves so that we silence the accuser of the brethren and number two, we have to demonstrate to God that we are going to view failures through the covenant of "Sure Mercy" and give ourselves space to redeem them. That means walking with the homosexual as long as he is willing to change. That means restoring the adulterer and the sexually broken so they can possess their own vessel in honor. Our goal in restoration is first consistent victory over sin, followed by resumption of duty in office, in call, and the anointing of the Holy Spirit to walk in their office and fulfill their call. It means extending ourselves and our reputation to walk with those who are broken so that the Redeemer can transform their lives and make them an example of His redemption! Cities and nations are waiting for the governmental anointing that God intended for the church to dispense. Why have we forfeited it so long by accusing and judging, when we could have been qualifying for an anointing that redeems cities and nations and releases terror on the terrorists?

How do you treat those
Who stumble and fall
Do you walk beside them
Through their failures and all

Do you have God's heart
To heal and restore
If so prepare, saint
God's bringing you <u>more</u>

More power to redeem
On a scale that is large
More holy anointing
To release and discharge

Chapter 7

The Transformational Power of Failure

David's moral failure occurs in Second Samuel 11. In chapter 12 he is confronted, repents, and walks through the eight steps of restoration. The failure transforms him into a minister of mercy. From this point on, he also becomes a dividing line. Prior to this David had gained a reputation as a premiere warrior, probably from his valiant disposition of the giant. David, as the killer of Goliath of Gath, had earned a reputation of being a mighty warrior. This extended to every area of his life. Not only on the battle field was he seen as a man of action, but also in his personal life. When he brought up the ark into the city of David he was accused of displaying indecent behavior. David did not respond with mercy. In First Chronicles 15:28–29 we are told:

> Thus all Israel brought up the ark of the covenant of the LORD with shouting and with the sound of the horn, with trumpets and with cymbals, making music with stringed instruments and harps. And it happened, as the ark of the covenant of the LORD came to the City of David, that Michal the daughter of Saul, looking through a window, saw King David whirling and playing music; and she despised him in her heart.

Second Samuel 6 records Michal's attitude toward David in verses 20–23:

> Then David returned to bless his household. And Michal the daughter of Saul came out to meet David, and said, "How glorious was the king of Israel today, uncovering himself today in the eyes of the maids of his servants, as one of the base fellows shamelessly uncovers himself!" So David said to Michal, "It was before the LORD, who chose me instead of your father and all his house, to appoint me ruler over the people of the LORD, over Israel. Therefore I will play music before the LORD. And I will be even more undignified than this, and will be humble in my own sight. But as for the maidservants of whom you have spoken, by them I will be held in honor." Therefore Michal the daughter of Saul had no children to the day of her death.

There are two possibilities for why Michal *"had no children to the day of her death."* One was God's direct hand of judgment on her but the other is because she may have been locked up never to see a man again. When we look at David the warrior, whether in his personal life or his leadership of God's army, we find a man who was decisive and quick to go to war. When David went to war, he displayed God's heart. He didn't leave anybody living. First Samuel 30 records David recovering all that was taken at Ziklag. Verse 17 says, *"And David attacked them from twilight until the evening of the next day. Not a man of them escaped, except four hundred young men who rode on camels and fled."* So we could say the kids got away, but that was about all. In the instance of Nabal we find another example of David's heart as a warrior. David sent to ask provisions for his men, because they had protected Nabal's flocks all the time they were together. Nabal answered David roughly.

In First Samuel 25:14–16 we're told:

Now one of the young men told Abigail, Nabal's wife, saying, 'Look, David sent messengers from the wilderness to greet our master; and he reviled them. But the men were very good to us, and we were not hurt, nor did we miss anything as long as we accompanied them, when we were in the fields. They were a wall to us both by night and day, all the time we were with them keeping the sheep.

David's response to Nabal is the response of a warrior. Verses 21–22 state:

Now David had said, 'Surely in vain I have protected all that this fellow has in the wilderness, so that nothing was missed of all that belongs to him. And he has repaid me evil for good. May God do so, and more also, to the enemies of David, if I leave one male of all who belong to him by morning light.

David was ready to go in and take the head off of every single male associated with Nabal. This reveals David *before* his failure. Looking at David *after* his failure with Bathsheba and Uriah the Hittite presents an entirely different picture. We almost have to conclude that David became a new man.

In Second Samuel 13 David's son Amnon rapes his daughter Tamar. Tamar has a brother named Absalom. David finds out about it. He gets very angry. David's mercy to Amnon becomes a yardstick by which Absalom is measured. Absalom refuses to extend mercy to Amnon and plots to have him killed. When Amnon is killed, all the king's sons flee, along with Absalom. Absalom refused the covenant of "Sure Mercy." That refusal brought an impact in four areas, based on Second Samuel 13:36–39:

So it was, as soon as he had finished speaking, that the king's sons indeed came, and they lifted up their voice and wept. Also the king and all his servants wept very bitterly. But Absalom fled and went to Tamai the son of Ammihud, king of Geshur. And David mourned for his son every day. So Absalom fled and went to Geshur, and was there three years. And King David longed to go to Absalom. For he had been comforted concerning Amnon, because he was dead.

Absalom's failure to heed "Sure Mercy" allowed unforgiveness to grow into bitterness. Absalom was very bitter over the mercy shown Amnon. The covenant of "Sure Mercy" has to be embraced and implemented or we reap the repercussions. The second area of impact was a three-year separation from his family. The third aspect was spiritual captivity which fell upon Absalom from which he never recovered. Absalom was a captive of bitterness and judgment toward David which ultimately resulted in his death. Finally, Absalom was locked away in exile. Only through David's mercy was Absalom brought home, but the seeds of captivity soon manifested anyway.

Everywhere David went the mercy he showed to others became a yardstick by which people were judged. Absalom was judged by the mercy that David showed Amnon, Absalom's refusal to deal with Amnon mercifully ended in a failed attempt to take David's throne. This conspiracy doomed every participant.

In Second Samuel 17:1–3 we're told, *"Moreover Ahithophel said to Absalom, 'Now let me choose twelve thousand men, and **I will** arise and pursue David tonight. **I will** come upon him while he is weary and weak, and make him afraid. And all the people who are with him will flee, and **I will** strike only the king. Then **I will** bring back all the people to you. When all return except the man whom you seek, then all the people will be at peace.'"* Ahithophel was the leading prophet in the land. Everything he said came to pass. In addition, Ahithophel was David's best friend. We have to ask ourselves why the four "***I will's***" of Second Samuel 17:1–3:

Ahithophel said, ". . . **I will** arise and pursue David tonight, **I will** come upon him while he is weary and weak, and make him afraid. And all the people who are with him will flee, and **I will** strike only the king. Then **I will** bring back all the people to you."

Something has eaten away at the friendship of David and Ahithophel. David even asked Hushai, the Archite, to stay back and try to thwart the good counsel of Ahithophel, which Hushai did. Interestingly enough, when Ahithophel found out Absalom had chosen Hushai's counsel, in verse 23 we are told, *"Now when Ahithophel saw that his counsel was not followed, he saddled his donkey, and arose and went home to his house, to his city. Then he put his household in order, and hanged himself, and died; and he was buried in his father's tomb."* He hanged himself and died because he saw David victorious and restored to the throne. What blinded his prophetic vision? **What** was the central issue?

In Second Samuel 23:34 the lineage of Ahithophel is revealed: *"Eliphelet the son of Ahasbai, the son of the Maacathite, Eliam the son of Ahithophel the Gilonite. . . ."* Ahithophel had a son named Eliam and according to Second Samuel 11:3, *"So David sent and inquired about the woman. And someone said, 'Is this not Bathsheba, the daughter of Eliam, the wife of Uriah the Hittite?'"* David did not just fool around with any stranger's granddaughter. He took his best friend, Ahithophel's own granddaughter to bed. Ahithophel chose not to forgive and not to extend mercy. Ahithophel died. If Ahithophel could have embraced the covenant of "Sure Mercy," he could have possibly impacted Solomon with his wisdom and passion for right and wrong! By refusing mercy to David, Ahithophel killed his greatest potential legacy—imparting what could have saved Solomon at the end of his reign. How could this be? Solomon desperately needed a piece of Ahithophel's heart. Generational impartation has a long biblical history.

How much legacy are we forfeiting by refusing covenant mercy? Amon chose not to extend mercy to Tamar when she cried out not to be sent away. Amon died. Absalom chose not to extend mercy. Absalom died. Joab was told to extend mercy to Abaslom, as the two armies battled. Joab refused. Joab died. Shimei cursed David and threw rocks. In the transition from David to Solomon's reign Shemei died. There is an emerging pattern that cannot be avoided. If we reject mercy, we die prematurely. First of all David was totally transformed by his failure. Failure made him a man of great mercy. Everywhere he displayed mercy, his example became a yardstick by which others were judged. Can we afford to refuse the covenant of "Sure Mercy"? If we want to move in the full measure of God's governmental authority in the last days, the covenant of "Sure Mercy" is our platform and it is time to embrace it.

There is a path through failure
On to victory
As David was . . . you will be forged
And exploits you will see

Chapter 8

Receiving Righteousness

Hebrews 10:12–22 invites every New Testament believer to come before the Throne in confidence. Verses 12–13 remind us that Jesus has been made to sit at the right hand of God *". . . waiting until His enemies are made His footstool."* Considering what God has done for the church in the process of salvation and redemption, verses 19–22 state:

> Therefore, brethren, having boldness to enter the Holiest by the blood of Jesus, by a new and living way which He consecrated for us, through the veil, that is, His flesh, and having a High Priest over the house of God, let us draw near with a true heart in full assurance of faith, having our hearts sprinkled from an evil conscience and our bodies washed with pure water. Let us hold fast the confession of our hope without wavering, for He who promised is faithful.

We are exhorted to *"draw near with a true heart in full assurance of faith."* The Greek word translated "full" is **play-rof-or-ee-ah**. The first half of the word comes from **play-race** meaning "to make full or to fill and make complete or to fill until no space remains." **For-eh-o** means "to have a burden or to wear as clothing or a constant companion." We are called to be *"full . . . of faith,"* which is a picture of walking in boldness before the Throne, as if we belonged there, and can access God's dominion as needed. It is impossible to take that posture without righteousness becoming a reality in our lives. In Romans 5:16–17 we are promised:

> And the gift is not like that which came through the one who sinned. For the judgment which came from one offense resulted in condemnation, but the free gift which came from many offenses resulted in justification. For if by the one man's offense death reigned through the one, much more those who receive abundance of grace and of the gift of righteousness will reign in life through the One, Jesus Christ.

We are invited to reign in life through righteousness. The question is, how does righteousness spend and bring forth the reign of God? In the first place, it is worthless unless it is received. Because only in the receiving is the boldness and access with confidence possible.

First Peter 2 sheds a little bit of light on this entire process in verses 1–4 when it states, *"Therefore, laying aside all malice, all guile, hypocrisy, envy, and all evil speaking, as newborn babes, desire the pure milk of the word, that you may grow thereby, if indeed you have tasted that the LORD is gracious. Coming to Him as to a living stone, rejected indeed by men, but chosen by God and precious. . . ."* If righteousness were presented as a door, the question would be how could we walk through it? It helps to be chosen, but verses 5–10 go on to describe the process:

> . . . you also, as living stones, are being built up a spiritual house, a holy priesthood, to offer up spiritual sacrifices acceptable to God through Jesus Christ. Therefore it is also contained in the

Scripture, "Behold, I lay in Zion A chief cornerstone, elect, precious, And he who believes on Him will by no means be put to shame." Therefore, to you who believe, He is precious; but to those who are disobedient, "The stone which the builders rejected Has become the chief cornerstone." And "A stone of stumbling And a rock of offense." They stumble, being disobedient to the word, to which they also were appointed. But you are a chosen generation, a royal priesthood, a holy nation, His own special people, that you may proclaim the praises of Him who called you out of darkness into His marvelous light; who once were not a people but are now the people of God, who had not obtained mercy but now have obtained mercy.

In this passage we have mercy presented as a door—a door into the Throne Room where we can go and present our petitions and call forth God's purposes. The covenant of "Sure Mercy" is that door and it is a door that leads to righteousness, redemption and confidence.

Second Samuel 7 records the fourth of the theocratic covenants (where God offers to reign through man). This covenant guarantees mercy which redeems the failure and makes it a platform on which we can stand and finish our calling. How we use it determines the level of confidence and overcoming displayed in our warfare with the accuser of the brethren. Whenever the enemy comes to accuse, thoughts of shame, accusation, and worthlessness arise. Our first line of defense should be the covenant of "Sure Mercy," because "Sure Mercy" guarantees forgiveness, justification, righteousness, redemption and confidence. We should be speaking it morning and evening until it becomes part of how we think, how we live and how we move. Walking through God's door of mercy releases a confidence that can be gained no other way, a confidence to boldly come before the Throne and obtain mercy and deliverance for others.

One path that leads to righteousness
And gives you holy confidence
Is God's Throne-room-mercy-door
Releasing boldness and much more

Chapter 9

How "Sure" Are "Sure Mercies"?

Acts 13:32–34 says:

> And we declare to you glad tidings—that promise which was
> made to the fathers. God has fulfilled this for us their children,
> in that He has raised up Jesus. As it is also written in the second
> Psalm: "You are My Son. Today I have begotten You." And that
> He raised Him from the dead, no more to return to corruption,
> He has spoken thus: "I will give you the sure mercies of David."

The question comes as to how **sure** are the sure mercies? In Paul's
understanding, they are bought and paid for by Jesus. They are active,
operational and fully accessible to all who believe. But the question
remains, do the sure mercies satisfy the sevenfold test of prophetic
doctrine? The sevenfold test is a standard the Holy Spirit gave that,
when satisfied, cements a spiritual foundation. This test solidifies our
confidence to the authenticity of a biblical truth, making it logical
and easy to believe.

Satisfying the sevenfold test is like pouring liquid cement that
forms into absolute unshakable confidence. The seven elements
are:

1. Does it appear in Genesis in seed form?
2. Can we find it apart from Genesis in the Pentateuch (first five books)?
3. Is it in Psalms or Proverbs?
4. Do we see it in the prophets?
5. Did Jesus teach it?
6. Is there an appearance of or reference to it in the book of Acts?
7. Do we see it in the epistles?

This sevenfold test of prophetic doctrine allows us to take a truth and when satisfied in all these areas, proclaim it with utter and complete authority knowing that it is a constant thread running through the entire Bible.

Because satan uses the spirit of mammon to gain his way with man opposing the work of the Holy Spirit, God has ordained an end–time judgment exposing and thwarting the results. The prophets saw an end–time transfer of wealth in which the unrighteous lost all their ill–gotten gain. During this season the Holy Spirit releases what we will call the "anointing to spoil." The "anointing to spoil" is a good theme with which to practice the sevenfold test to see if it really measures up. For an in–depth discussion of the "anointing to spoil," see the book *Purifying the Altar.* "Prosperity" and "wealth transfer" have been presented by many preachers as an "end–time promise" just waiting for those with enough "faith" to believe them into existence, and are usually promised as a result of sowing into the proclaiming individual's ministry. I look forward to the day when the least discerning saint can spot the spiritual pimps who promise great things but pervert God's Word by omitting the preparational price so they can sell more material. Taking a biblical truth and corrupting it through a spirit of mammon by indiscriminately promising it to everyone who gives does not negate the promise. Such actions insulate the church from truth of Scripture by polluting it with manipulation, so that good people discard it as tainted doctrine! The enemy always sends counterfeits, preceding the real, to muddy the water, cloud the issue and insulate the church against God's purposes. Satisfying the sevenfold test can help restore what the enemy has stolen!

If the "anointing to spoil" were to pass the sevenfold test, it would have to appear in all seven places. We would have to start by finding it in Genesis, then tracing it through each test to the Epistles. Genesis 14:20 is the account of Abraham arming his servants and going to war for the goods of Sodom and Gomorrah when all their provisions and people were taken captive. Abraham gained it all back, including Lot and his family. So we see the anointing to spoil first manifested in Genesis by warfare. In Genesis 26, God intervened specifically in a season of famine and told Isaac not to make the same generational mistake his father initiated in a time of famine by running to Egypt. He was encouraged rather to stay in the midst of famine and plant a crop expecting a supernatural harvest. In Genesis 26:12–13, he received a hundredfold return. So we discover the "anointing to spoil" can also come via sowing and reaping. And finally in Genesis 49:27 Jacob's blessing of Benjamin states, *"Benjamin is a ravenous wolf; In the morning he shall devour the prey, And at night he shall divide the spoil."* So it can also come via a spiritual or physical inheritance. While our test only requires one example, we find the "anointing to spoil" in three different places in seed form in Genesis. God must really be committed to this principal!

The second test is, "Does it appear in the Law?" Deuteronomy 20:14–15 declare:

> But the women, the little ones, the livestock, and all that is in the city, all its spoil, you shall plunder for yourself; and you shall eat the enemies' plunder which the LORD your God gives you. Thus you shall do to all the cities which are very far from you, which

are not of the cities of these nations. But of the cities of these peoples which the LORD your God gives you as an inheritance, you shall let nothing that breathes remain alive.

It seems like the very same God who sent Saul on a mission to annihilate the Amalekites also demanded that Israel completely and totally cleanse the cities they were possessing, because those cities had been filled with iniquity and the land was vomiting out the inhabitants. Spoil became the Law of Conquest.

Does it appear in Psalms or Proverbs? Psalm 68:11–12 declares, *"The LORD gave the word; Great was the company of those who proclaimed it: Kings of armies flee, they flee, And she who remains at home* **divides the spoil.**" We find it in the Psalms.

Did the prophets proclaim a season where God would bring wealth into believers' hands for His end-time purposes? The answer to that appears in Isaiah 60:5. It says, *"Then you shall see and become radiant, And your heart shall swell with joy; Because the abundance of the sea shall be turned to you,* **The wealth of the Gentiles shall come to you.**"

The prophets proclaimed it!

Did Jesus teach it? In Matthew 12:22–29 He certainly did. In Matthew 12:27–29 Jesus put it this way:

And if I cast out demons by Beelzebub, by whom do your sons cast them out? Therefore they shall be your judges. But if I cast out demons by the Spirit of God, surely the kingdom of God has come upon you. Or else how can one enter a strong man's house and plunder his goods, unless he first binds the strong man? And then **he will plunder** his house.

If we look at two passages utilizing **har-paz-o**, the power that Jesus pours through the church to spoil the enemy in the last days exceeds what is demonstrated by the rapture. Two Greek words convey the picture of taking for yourself what another has. **Klep-to** means to sneak off with something in the dark where hardly anyone can see the theft. A **klep-to** done in the daylight executes the classic "snatch and grab," while **har-paz-o,** on the other hand, means to seize or overpower forcefully where all can see as a demonstration of superior power and strength. The prefix **dia** is added when we want to convey a dramatic increase or even doubling of the demonstration of a simple **har-paz-o.** We could all probably agree, the rapture constitutes a significant demonstration of power. In First Thessalonians 4:17 the Greek word for "caught up" is **har-paz-o.** The word that is used in Matthew 12:29 translated *"he will plunder"* is a strengthened form of that word, **dia-har-paz-o.** When we compare these two events, based on strength of language, what God pours *through* the church will exceed in demonstration what is released when He takes the church *up* in the rapture. The greatest rapture is what the church does to demonstrate God's wisdom to principalities and powers. Will the government of God please rise!

The church has to demonstrate the power of God to presidents and prime ministers in the last days, proving God's wisdom! Because satan uses mammon like God uses the Holy Spirit, God has ordained and prophesied consistently from Genesis to Revelation that He will execute an end–time judgment on what the enemy has stored up, releasing it to pay for the discipling of nations! The mineral wealth of the Muslim mammonites, the gold of the Gentiles, the silver of the satanists belongs to the church and it must be possessed through the government of God and the anointing of the Holy Spirit. The church probably won't be **har-paz-o** (raptured) until we fulfill our purpose and demonstrate **dia-har-paz-o** exploits to principalities and powers in a dramatic international harvest. The greatest days of the church are ahead!

Do we find a manifestation of the "anointing to spoil" in the book of Acts? Acts 4:32–35 is an account of people selling their properties and bringing the money and laying it at the apostles' feet by divine direction. In the process of doing this they brought new measures of the government of God into manifestation and they demonstrated God's wisdom to principalities and powers.

Finally we need to see these truths mentioned in the epistles. James 5:1–9 exhorts us to wait on the Lord because He has ordained the anointing to spoil for the end–times. Verses 1–4 state:

> Come now, you rich, weep and howl for your miseries that are coming upon you! Your riches are corrupted, and your garments are moth–eaten. Your gold and silver are corroded, and their corrosion will be a witness against you and will eat your flesh like fire. You have heaped up treasure in the last days. Indeed the wages of the laborers who mowed your fields, which you kept back by fraud, cry out; and the cries of the reapers have reached the ears of the Lord of Sabaoth.

Verse 4 enumerates the key to releasing this dramatic judgment. The cries of ministers who have no resources to match the burden of vision God has given come before the Throne demanding a financial judgment. Imagine Hollywood icons losing their money to the church which they continually hate and constantly denigrate. What a glorious day that will be! Verses 5–9 conclude:

> You have lived on the earth in pleasure and luxury; you have fattened your hearts as in a day of slaughter. You have condemned, you have murdered the just; he does not resist you. Therefore be patient, brethren, until the coming of the Lord. See how the farmer waits for the precious fruit of the earth, waiting patiently for it until it receives the early and latter rain. You also be patient. Establish your hearts, for the coming of the Lord is at hand. Do not

grumble against one another, brethren, lest you be condemned. Behold, the Judge is standing at the door!

God is going to execute judgment on mammon. The mammonites are going to lose their money. Wealth–transfer consistently meets the sevenfold test of doctrine. The problem, of course, is in **how** it has been taught. **It hasn't been taught with the integrity of the cross.** Prominent preachers promise riches and wealth to people indiscriminately. Wealth–transfer is a judgment on the spirit of mammon. The **laws that govern judgments** demand that if we participate in executing judgment for the Lord, the spirit of mammon can have no place in us. The wealth that is possessed in the end–times is not to be spent on the whims of individuals. This money has to be spent for Kingdom purposes, therefore it demands that a level of preparation come upon every individual who qualifies. One must be delivered from the spirit of mammon to execute judgment on that spirit. If you volunteer to participate in executing God's promise, welcome to a preparational Boot Camp that is like no other.

How **sure** is "Sure Mercy"? Is it as sure as the "anointing to spoil"? Can we find "Sure Mercy" in Genesis so that we know it is indeed consistently **sure** and a theme that marches throughout Scripture? We certainly can. In Genesis 19:15–16 we find:

> When the morning dawned, the angels urged Lot to hurry, saying, "Arise, take your wife and your two daughters who are here, lest you be consumed in the punishment of the city." And while he lingered, the men took hold of his hand, his wife's hand, and the hands of his two daughters, the LORD being merciful to him, and they brought him out and **set him** outside the city.

Of all the times to linger, Lot picked the worst, but God demonstrated mercy. In the middle of destroying Sodom and Gomorrah,

God extended mercy to Lot and his family. We can really make a case for the fact they didn't really deserve it. But He extended it for one reason—Abraham asked for it. Abraham stood before the Lord and said, *"Should not the God of all the earth do right?"* He actually put it this way in Genesis 18:24–25:

> Suppose there were fifty righteous within the city; would You also destroy the place and not spare it for the fifty righteous that were in it? Far be it from You to do such a thing as this, to slay the righteous with the wicked, so that the righteous should be as the wicked; far be it from You! Shall not the Judge of all the earth do right?

God said, "Yes," He would do right. And we know Abraham persuaded God to spare the city for ten. The problem was, He couldn't find ten. Such is the power and perversion of homosexuality and lesbianism to destroy a culture when it is allowed to function and operate. Our forefathers understood that and made sexual perversion illegal. It needs to be made illegal again in America, because the consistent truth of Scripture states if you statutorily protect perversion at that magnitude, it defiles the land and fills it with iniquity until judgment comes and you can no longer protect the nation or land you have been given! Leviticus 20:22–23 states the fruit of homosexuality:

> You shall therefore keep all My statutes and all My judgments, and perform them, that the land where I am bringing you to dwell may not vomit you out. And you shall not walk in the statutes of the nation which I am casting out before you; for they commit all these things, and therefore I abhor them."

The covenant of "Sure Mercy" is **sure** in Genesis. It was so **sure** it got

Lot and his family delivered when they weren't "sure" they wanted to go. Mercy prevailed over judgment!

In Deuteronomy 7:12–13 we see "Sure Mercy" in the Law. Verses 12–13 state:

> Then it shall come to pass, because you listen to these judgments, and keep and do them, that the LORD your God will keep with you the covenant and the mercy which He swore to your fathers. And He will love you and bless you and multiply you; He will also bless the fruit of your womb and the fruit of your land, your grain and your new wine and your oil, the increase of your cattle and the offspring of your flock, in the land of which He swore to your fathers to give you.

The promise in the Law is that if you "do God's Word" He will keep His covenant and mercy with you. It is plain for all to see. It is as clear as it can be. In chapter 7, verses 8–9 the Scripture says this:

> . . . but because the LORD loves you, and because He would keep the oath which He swore to your fathers, the LORD has brought you out with a mighty hand, and redeemed you from the house of bondage, from the hand of Pharaoh king of Egypt. Therefore know that the LORD your God, He is God, the faithful God who keeps covenant **and mercy for** a thousand generations with those who love Him and keep His commandments.

The Law, even though it required action, also promised covenant mercy. We ask ourselves, Do we find "Sure Mercy" in the Psalms or Proverbs? In Psalm 51 David, in the midst of his greatest failure—adultery with Bathsheba and the murder of Uriah the Hittite—cries out, *"Have mercy upon me, O God, According to Your lovingkindness; According to the multitude of Your tender mercies, Blot out my trans-*

gressions in verse 11, *"Do not cast me away from Your presence, And do not take Your Holy Spirit from me."* He has good reason to pray that because God had taken the Holy Spirit from Saul who was before him. David knows his covenant of "Sure Mercy." David prays his covenant of "Sure Mercy." He asks to keep the anointing to walk in the office and fulfill the call. God honors the covenant! Psalms proclaims "Sure Mercy"!

Does "Sure Mercy" appear in the prophets? Isaiah 55:1–3 declares, *"Incline your ear, and come to Me. Hear, and your soul shall live; And I will make an everlasting covenant with you—the sure mercies of David."* The prophets proclaim "Sure Mercy"!

Did Jesus teach it? It is in Matthew 12:1–8:

At that time Jesus went through the grainfields on the Sabbath. And His disciples were hungry, and began to pluck heads of grain and to eat. But when the Pharisees saw it, they said to Him, "Look, Your disciples are doing what is not lawful to do on the Sabbath!" Then He said to them, "Have you not read what David did when he was hungry, he and those who were with him: how he entered the house of God and ate the showbread which was not lawful for him to eat, nor for those who were with him, but only for the priests? Or have you not read in the law that on the Sabbath the priests in the temple profane the Sabbath, and are blameless? But I say to you that in this place there is One greater than the temple. But if you had known what this means, 'I desire mercy and not sacrifice,' you would not have condemned the guiltless. For the Son of Man is Lord even of the Sabbath.

Jesus desired mercy and not sacrifice. If we understand that, we refrain from condemning the guiltless. Jesus taught "Sure Mercy"! Extending mercy horizontally qualifies us to activate the covenant vertically over a city or nation.

Do we find the covenant of "Sure Mercy" in the book of Acts? Yes, it is in Acts 13:33–34. It was the message that came out of the Antioch church, and perhaps it is the reason why the Antioch church defied tradition and became multicultural. It probably forms the foundation for believers being first called Christians!

Finally, do we find it in the epistles? We certainly do and once again the crowning achievement comes from James 2 where he says in verses 12–13, *"So speak and so do as those who will be judged by the law of liberty. For judgment is without mercy to the one who has shown no mercy. Mercy triumphs over judgment."*

How **sure** is the **covenant of "Sure Mercy"?** It is so sure that even Jeremiah prophesied about it. In Jeremiah 33:20–21 Jeremiah says this:

> **Thus says the LORD: 'If you can break My covenant with the day and My covenant with the night, so that there will not be day and night in their season, then My covenant may also be broken with David My servant, so that he shall not have a son to reign on his throne, and with the Levites, the priests, My ministers.**

If we ever arise in the morning and find a day where the sun has not risen in the east to go down in the west, *then* we can say that the covenant of "Sure Mercy" is broken. But as long as the sun rises and sets, the very sun is a testimony to the power of the covenant of "Sure Mercy" and is given to every believer to stand and minister in behalf of his family, his city and his nation. The **covenant of "Sure Mercy"** is perhaps as **sure** as God Himself. It certainly is as **sure** as the creation. Statements like Jeremiah made are made for one reason and the reason is so we can know that we *know* that we **know** that we have a covenant to stand on that cannot be broken. Such statements are made to give us confidence in the Throne Room.

As sure as the creation
And the rising of the sun
God's mercy is that sure to you
It's benefits you've won

A covenant unbroken
That declares beyond a doubt
That what your God has guaranteed
Will surely come about

Chapter 10

How Do We Use "Sure Mercy"?

If the covenant of "Sure Mercy" is so good that the only way to stop it is to violate the laws of creation so that the sun does not rise and set, then we know it must have a strategic and major purpose for the end–time church. Perhaps the most functional preparational purpose first appears in Revelation 12 where we find the true nature of our warfare. Verses 10–11 tell us:

> Then I heard a loud voice saying in heaven, "Now salvation, and strength, and the kingdom of our God, and the power of His Christ have come, for the accuser of our brethren, who accused them before our God day and night, has been cast down. And they overcame him by the blood of the Lamb and by the word of their testimony, and they did not love their lives to the death."

If we fast–forward to verse 17 we find this statement, *"And the dragon was enraged with the woman, and he went to make war with the rest of her offspring, who keep the commandments of God and have the testimony of Jesus Christ."*

Scripture consistently tells us that there is an accusatory war that comes against every person who names the Name of Jesus. That war is in our mind and constantly comes against us to try and destroy our confidence in the Throne Room. The *"accuser of the brethren"* makes his initial assault individually upon every believer.

Second Corinthians 10:3–6 says:

> For though we walk in the flesh, we do not war according to the flesh. For the weapons of our warfare are not carnal but mighty in God for pulling down strongholds, casting down arguments and every high thing that exalts itself against the knowledge of God, bringing every thought into captivity to the obedience of Christ, and being ready to punish all disobedience when your obedience is fulfilled.

The very first application of the covenant of "Sure Mercy" is to destroy the accusations of the enemy against us in our own mind. We have to take that covenant and remind the enemy that God has promised to make our greatest failures the platform for our greatest success. We use it to silence the accuser—personally. Then we can go on and take a stand on that covenant and use it for others, either our family, our church, our city, or our nation. We then can use it corporately and we are obviously encouraged to do so. When Paul taught the covenant of "Sure Mercy" in Acts 13, he went on to warn what would happen if it was not incorporated and used to stand in the gap for our cities and our nation. In Acts 13:34–40 we find the unfolding of this warning:

> And that He raised Him from the dead, no more to return to corruption, He has spoken thus: "I will give you the sure mercies of David" Therefore He also says in another Psalm: "You will not allow Your Holy One to see corruption." For David, after he had served his own generation by the will of God, fell asleep,

was buried with his fathers, and saw corruption; but He whom God raised up saw no corruption. Therefore let it be known to you, brethren, that through this Man is preached to you the forgiveness of sins; and by Him everyone who believes is justified from all things from which you could not be justified by the law of Moses. Beware therefore, lest what has been spoken in the prophets come upon you.

In verse 40 Paul tells us to *"Beware therefore, lest what has been spoken in the prophets come upon you. . . ."* Context always determines meaning. Context determines application of the covenant of "Sure Mercy." All we have to do is go find the verse in the prophets that Paul uses and look at the quote in its context. If the context of Acts 13:41 is in the destruction of a city, or the destruction of a nation, then we know precisely what Paul is saying to us. We must accept the covenant of "Sure Mercy" and begin to use it for our city and then for our nation, because if we don't we can lose both. It just so happens that Acts 13:41 appears twice in the Old Testament. It appears first in Isaiah 29:1–4, 11–16. In verses 1–4 the prophet is speaking a warning to Ariel the city of David. The city of David is Jerusalem. He goes on to say in verses 11–14:

The whole vision has become to you like the words of a book that is sealed, which men deliver to one who is literate, saying, "Read this, please"; and he says, "I cannot, for it is sealed." Then the book is delivered to one who is illiterate, saying, "Read this, please"; and he says, "I am not literate." Therefore the LORD said: "Inasmuch as these people draw near to Me with their mouths And honor Me with their lips, But have removed their hearts far from Me, And their fear toward Me is taught by the commandment of men, Therefore, behold, I will again **do a marvelous work** among this people, **A marvelous work and a wonder**; For the wisdom of their wise men shall perish, And the understanding of their prudent men shall be hidden."

Isaiah prophesied the loss of Jerusalem if Israel did not take to heart repentance and turning. So Paul reaches back, by the Holy Spirit, to a verse in which God says He will do a marvelous work and a wonder and that work is judgment. The whole city will be removed and go into captivity. So it is obvious in context that Paul is saying to actively use the covenant of "Sure Mercy." Use it for your city or face the potential loss of that city!

The final appearance of this Scripture is in Habakkuk 1. In Habakkuk 1:1–7 the warning is for the loss of the nation. It says God is raising up the Chaldeans and they are going to execute judgment against the nation of Israel. It is obvious that Paul understood the power of the covenant of "Sure Mercy" and he understood it from Abram's intercession concerning Lot all the way through Isaiah to the fullness in Christ. He understood the covenant of "Sure Mercy" that became part of David's temple. The covenant of "Sure Mercy" belongs to us and if we can confidently use it for ourselves, then we can confidently go into the Throne Room and make an impact slowing or stopping the judgments on our cities. The reason for stopping the judgment is gaining a greater harvest. In a season when Muslim terrorists are pursuing nuclear weapons with the sole purpose of attacking America or completely destroying Israel, hundreds of thousands of lives hang in the balance.

Isaiah went on to promise that when the world sees the church moving in "Sure Mercy" whole nations would run to us. The God of mercy is far different in His treatment of failure than the god of Islam who demands lopping off heads and hands.

The world is waiting to see a church moving in the **covenant of "Sure Mercy."**

In personal warfare
You must learn to stand
Against the destruction
The enemy's planned

All those accusations
Deceptions and lies
Cripple your walk
And God's purpose defies

Through personal victory
You move up the line
Gaining even nations
By divine design

Chapter 11

Agents of Restoration

Acts 3:19–21 states:

> Repent therefore and be converted, that your sins may be blotted out, so that times of refreshing may come from the presence of the Lord, and that He may send Jesus Christ, who was preached to you before, whom heaven must receive until the times of restoration of all things, which God has spoken by the mouth of all His holy prophets since the world began.

This passage highlights the coming of the Lord for an empowering, as opposed to what most of us have been schooled to think the "coming of the Lord" means in terms of being caught away in the rapture. There are three distinct "comings" of the Lord presented in the New Testament. The last one is in Jude 14 which says:

> Now Enoch, the seventh from Adam, prophesied about these men also, saying, "Behold, the Lord comes **with** ten thousands of His saints, to execute judgment on all, to convict all who are ungodly among them of all their ungodly deeds which they have

committed in an ungodly way, and of all the harsh things which ungodly sinners have spoken against Him."

This coming of the Lord is with finality, with judgment and **with** the saints.

Prior to the final "with the saints" coming, we have First Thessalonians 4:17 which is "**for**" the saints. Verse 17 says, *"Then we who are alive and remain shall be **caught up** together with them in the clouds to meet the Lord in the air. And thus we shall always be with the Lord."* This coming is "**for**" the saints and commonly known as the "rapture."

However, when we come to Acts 3 this is an entirely different "coming" with a very pointed purpose. This "coming" has a divine purpose that the church must be empowered to fulfill. Verses 20–21 say:

> . . . and that He may send Jesus Christ, who was preached **to you** before, whom heaven must receive until the times [plural—more than one] of restoration of all things, which God has spoken by the mouth of all His holy prophets since the world began.

Jesus has the end–time assignment of coming **to** the church to empower it to fulfill what the prophets promised. The greatest days of the church are ahead. We need to prepare to meet Jesus who is coming to empower us to fulfill all that the Father has in mind for the end–time church. The first two questions that arise are, What will this visitation look like, and How long will it last?

We know that God spreads every major prophetic transition over two generations. Moses brought the people out of Egypt, but it took Joshua to take them into the promised land. David secured all the architectural and operational plans for the temple, including placement of the storage rooms. He used his faith and accumulated all the material through the anointing to spoil needed for completion.

David could not build the temple. Solomon, of the next generation, had to build it. When Jesus came among men, He schooled them for three and a half years. Those who walked with Him tasted the apostolic culture, caught His heart, and received His anointing. But it took Paul, as one who came from the following generation, to finish the New Testament. Paul had to complete the revelation of all that Jesus had accomplished. We can also expect the end–time harvest will be spread over two generations. Just as it took two donkeys—parent and offspring—to transport Jesus into Jerusalem the first time, He will return on the backs of two generations. It is time to accept the Davidic pattern of preparation and fulfillment so that we can fully provide all that is needed for the completion of the spiritual temple erected in the last days with new and living stones. As we pass the torch, the anointing and the money to disciple nations will release the next generation. There is a Davidic call on our generation and we are challenged to say "yes" to it.

A very unique compound Greek word is used for "restoration." It is the word **ap-ok-at-as-tas-is. Apo** means "to remove or lift off with surgical skill." **Kath-is-tay-mee** means "to reposition, to set, or place in office, to set or place in a new condition." Restoration implies failure. Without a failure there is nothing to restore. So if the Lord makes us agents of restoration, then we know our chief job is among failures. How do we restore a failure? **Kath-is-tay-mee** means "to reposition, to set, or place in office in brand new condition." While restoration implies failure, we get to practice on the church before God allows us to take it to the world. Genesis 20:1 outlines a repeat failure with Abraham. This incident is the second time he made the same errant choice. He was told to go to Canaan, to stay in the land that God had given him, a land flowing with milk and honey. But there happened to be a famine in the land the first time he arrived. Instead of staying and trusting God to take care of him, Genesis 20:1 says, *"And Abraham journeyed from there to the*

South, and dwelt between Kadesh and Shur, and sojourned in Gerar." Every time Abram went south, Sarah paid the price by winding up in another man's tent. I'm sure Sarah became weary of this pattern. In Genesis 12, right after God had called Abraham to leave his culture and kindred to go to Canaan, we find the very same thing happening in verses 9–10 which state, *"So Abram journeyed, going on still toward the South. Now there was a famine in the land, and Abram went down to Egypt to sojourn there, for the famine was severe in the land."* God brought Abram to a land of promise that looked like a barren, worthless, famine–plagued desert wasteland. In both incidents, because Abram ran, God had to show up and rebuke those who had taken Sarah. In the process we see a word used which becomes the favorite word of the prophets in the Old Testament. In Genesis 20:7 we find this:

> Now therefore, **restore** the man's wife; for he is a prophet, and he will pray for you and you shall live. But if you do not **restore** her, know that you shall surely die, you and all who are yours.

The Hebrew word for "restore" is the word **sh-oob. Sh-oob** means "to turn around, come back, reverse direction or return to the point of departure." In order to prepare a vessel for restoration, the depth and magnitude of failure you encounter enhances and determines the depth and magnitude of restoration you can minister. Those who have experienced the greatest failures, according to the covenant of "Sure Mercies," are indeed the very ones with the greatest potential for ministries of restoration. For those caught in addictive behaviors, let the father of faith be your example. God delivered Abraham from his reoccurring failures. He will deliver you!

The alternate version of Job 36:15 gives credence to this principle. It says, *"He delivers the poor in their affliction, And opens their ears in oppression.—He delivers the afflicted by their affliction, and opens their ears to His voice by adversity."* The issue in failure has never been whether or not we deserve what comes. Of course we deserve judgment, but the covenant of "Sure Mercy" promises that if we will turn to God, He will redeem that failure and turn it into a platform for accomplishment. Only God could make such an offer to man.

In Jonah 1:11–15 we see God's hand in the midst of a very strong failure. Jonah refused to go preach what God ordered:

> Then they said to him, "What shall we do to you that the sea may be calm for us?"—for the sea was growing more tempestuous. And he said to them, "Pick me up and throw me into the sea; then the sea will become calm for you. For I know that the great tempest is because of me." Nevertheless the men rowed hard to bring the ship to land, but they could not, for the sea continued to grow more tempestuous against them. Therefore they cried out to the LORD and said, "We pray, O LORD, please do not let us perish for this man's life, and do not charge us with innocent blood; for You, O LORD, have done as it pleased You." So they picked up Jonah and threw him into the sea, and the sea ceased from its raging.

It is obvious that Jonah deserved the adversity that came, but what about all those on board with him? His presence affected many lives. Do all Americans deserve what abortion is bringing upon the land? Do all Americans deserve the judgment due a land that promotes perversion when federal courts overturn laws that states pass? In chapter 2, verse 1, we are told, *"Then Jonah prayed to the LORD his God from the fish's belly."* The men took Jonah at his word. They threw him into the water and the raging water stopped. They became instant believers. In verses 7–9 we are told:

> When my soul fainted within me, I remembered the LORD; And my prayer went up to You, Into Your holy temple. Those who

regard worthless idols Forsake their own Mercy. But I will sacrifice to You With the voice of thanksgiving; I will pay what I have vowed. Salvation is of the LORD.

When we read the account of Jonah, he is quoted as saying, *"Out of hell I cried."* Jonah 2:2 demonstrates exactly what Jonah felt like as he cried from inside the whale. He cried from hell. *"Out of the belly of Sheol I cried, And You heard my voice."* When we get down to verses 7, 8, and 9, Jonah talks about the issue of mercy and how mercy operates and functions. When Jonah declared mercy, restoration came. In chapter 3, verse 1, we discover one of the most encouraging words in the Bible for anyone who has ever had a failure, *"Now the word of the LORD came to Jonah the second time, saying, 'Arise, go to Nineveh, that great city, and preach to it the message that I tell you.'"* Will the word of the Lord come to us a second or third time? I suspect it will and the issue is because of the **covenant of "Sure Mercy."** When we are willing to use our faith to walk with people long enough to identify and cut off the diseased part and then pick them up and reposition them in God to go on and fulfill their ministry, then what Isaiah promised we will surely see. Nations will come to us and kings to the brightness of our rising. The other part of that is, what happens if we dishonor the covenant of "Sure Mercy" and refuse to extend it? We have already looked at a variety of people who found themselves in that place. Absalom was one, Ahithophel another, with Joab and Shimei fully qualifying. It is common to see it today. God wants the church to be agents of restoration. Agents of restoration cut off the diseased part so healing can begin. Picking people up and repositioning them to finish their gifting and calling carries an eternal reward. If we will practice on each other instead of judging, condemning and withdrawing from fellowship, then we will qualify to disciple nations and fulfill what the prophets promised.

Psalm 2 may well be the deciding factor for the church of the last days. Jesus bought and paid for nations and in Psalm 2 we are encouraged to ask. Verses 8–9 declare, *"Ask of Me, and I will give You the nations for Your inheritance, And the ends of the earth for Your possession. You shall break them with a rod of iron; You shall dash them in pieces like a potter's vessel."* The covenant of "Sure Mercy" promises the anointing to restore, reposition, and send people off to fulfill their gifting and calling. It is time we started practicing because the key to the end–time harvest is at stake. The covenant of "Sure Mercy" may well be the defining distinction in the transition from the Jerusalem church to the Antioch church. Paul had a revelation of the covenant of "Sure Mercy." He preached it in Acts 13. It is obvious he already had given that input to the Antioch church, thus accounting for their distinctively different flavor. Antioch was where they were first called Christians. It became a multicultural church, unlike Jerusalem who allowed Jews only. True team ministry was birthed out of Antioch where in Christ Jesus there was neither bond nor free, male nor female, Jew nor Greek! "Sure Mercy" was the platform.

An end-time harvest is at stake
Decisions count that God's saints make
Restore, position, and set free
"Sure Mercy" is a vital key

Part II

Imprecatory Mercies

Walking with Jesus the Judge

WARNING
The following principles are to be practiced only by mature
believers and intercessors in conjunction with Prophetic or
Pastoral approval and oversight.

Chapter 12

Graduating from Boot Camp

The church is in a war that intensifies year by year. Because we've had fifty years of Jesus the Savior preached, hardly anyone knows how to walk with Jesus the Judge. A Spiritual Boot Camp would really help "fast–forward" the church preparationally. Military Boot Camp is a shocking but necessary experience in wartime.

I will never forget my entry into Boot Camp. My last normal meal was at a Whataburger in Pensacola, Florida. I checked into Officer Candidate School, was promptly greeted with having all my hair cut off and issued the grossest green suit imaginable. For the next twelve weeks I belonged to Marine drill instructors because I was in Boot Camp! Please consider the next ten chapters as a Spiritual Boot Camp for representing Jesus the Judge. We need to get in shape to fight, using our most powerful weapons. It takes courage to fight a war. We must believe in what we are fighting for. Our goal is to regain lost salt so the church of our generation can impact society as the early church impacted theirs.

The early church developed a "Kingdom culture" from walking with the King! Once this warrior culture is recovered and the church regains its salt, we can move on to a harvest of nations. In Matthew 5:13, Jesus said, *"You are the salt of the earth; but if the salt loses its flavor, how shall it be seasoned? It is then good for nothing but to be thrown out and trampled under foot by men."* The phrase *"good for nothing"* gives a big clue from the Greek word used, as to the picture Jesus is portraying. The Greek word translated "good" is **is-khoo-o** describing the third of four levels of power. **Doo-nam-is** is the elementary entry level associated with the gifts of the Spirit. **Ex-oo-see-ah** is used for authority, as manifested in spiritual and political government. **Is-khoo-o** is the power needed when the demonized ascend to positions of power threatening the stability of a nation or when the godly have expended everything and can barely take one more step. The fourth level is dominion, when dominion is manifested, it turns every advance of the enemy into a rout guaranteeing victory. The picture presented in James 5 is of Elijah initiating the process by three and one–half long years of praying heaven shut. Then he confronted and killed the prophets of Baal. Even praying for rain to complete the assignment was a struggle. He prayed once—no cloud. He prayed again—no cloud. He prayed a third, fourth, fifth, sixth, and finally the seventh time before a cloud the size of a man's hand appeared. James 5:16 says, *"Confess your trespasses to one another, and pray for one another, that you may be healed. The effective, fervent prayer of a righteous man* [**is-khoo-ei**] ***avails much.***" Transparency is absolutely essential to qualify for and maintain (**is-khoo-o**) overcoming power. Through faith and obedience, Elijah overcame the perverting, defiling actions of Israel's national leaders. The people returned to the Lord.

Having salt means overcoming the perverting cultural influences and whatever branch of government that attempts to legislate them. Elijah had such an assignment for Israel. He prayed the heavens closed for three and one–half years. When he prayed, fire consumed the sacrifice and the people turned back to God. He prayed again and a hand appeared signifying rain. If the church can't move God's hand, then it has no salt. The hand of judgment has to come first so that the hand of blessing can produce rain. Let the salt be restored! The church must move God's hand! The culture of the Kingdom must be reestablished in the church. A church that cannot move God's hand in judgment and restoration is a church without salt.

If Jesus were to visit the church today, I believe He would speak the same word to many of us in ministry that He spoke in Matthew 23:23:

> Woe to you, scribes and Pharisees, hypocrites! For you pay tithe of mint and anise and cumin, and have neglected the weightier matters of the law; justice [or judgment] and mercy and faith. These you ought to have done, without leaving the others undone.

Jesus rebuked the Pharisees for neglecting the hard issues while blessing their teaching on the tithe. The tough issues are *"judgment, mercy, and faith."* A church that is incapable of "moving God's hand" in judgment will never approach the level of faith that was normative for the early church. The prophets have promised that those who wind up the age will do so with the *". . . former and latter rain in the same season."* We should double what the early church experienced. Most Christians view warfare like they view the U. S. military—a completely volunteer service. The fruit of such thinking is a church that has missed Spiritual Boot Camp.

As leaders, we have not made a priority of training disciples to walk with Jesus the Judge! Judgment is being discounted in many sectors of the church. It seems that a significant portion of ministers have trouble discerning the judgment of God in our midst. They call it "the natural course of events," or "these are things that just happen." If we don't develop the faith and the sensitivity to the

Spirit to know when to minister mercy and when to agree with the Spirit of Judgment, then we have not attained to the place where the early church walked. The early church did not view mercy and judgment as mutually exclusive. Peter had the faith to move with either, depending on where the Holy Spirit led. Today's church has faith for mercy but hardly any for judgment. If the church were a car, our tires would be so out of balance on this issue we could hardly drive. We desperately need military training! Understanding the interaction of judgment, mercy and faith are absolutely essential in completing a successful **Spiritual Boot Camp.** A successful graduate will have equal faith for judgment as for mercy so the Holy Spirit can push either direction.

Matthew 24:7a tells us, *"For nation will rise against nation, and kingdom against kingdom."* Since we are fighting a spiritual kingdom of darkness that wants to kill and annihilate everyone who is a Jew or who is a Christian, the issue of judgment is no longer optional. How can we gain the harvest God promised when we face this kind of warfare? Paul warned the church of what was coming.

Second Timothy 3:1–8 says:

> But know this, that in the last days perilous times will come: For men will be lovers of themselves, lovers of money, boasters, proud, blasphemers, disobedient to parents, unthankful, unholy, unloving, unforgiving, slanderers, without self–control, brutal, despisers of good, traitors, headstrong, haughty, lovers of pleasure rather than lovers of God, having a form of godliness but denying its power. And from such people turn away! For of this sort are those who creep into households and make captives of gullible women loaded down with sins, led away by various lusts, always learning and never able to come to the knowledge of the truth. Now as Jannes and Jambres resisted Moses, so do these also resist the truth; men of corrupt minds, disapproved concerning the faith.

The demonized resistance to biblical truth has grown dramatically. One national organization attempts to silence any expression of the church in the public arena! Their strategy seems to be to pervert the law through liberal Supreme Court Justices, utterly silencing the voice of the church. When analyzing the origin of the ACLU, coupled with a consistent thread of "silence the church" cases, how can a thoughtful person come to any other conclusion? How should the church respond? God's desire is that we maintain the freedom to speak the truth, while supernaturally responding to the demonically empowered, as when Moses faced off with Jannes and Jambres. God has promised a boundary for the demonized: *". . . But they will progress no further, for their folly will be manifest to all, as theirs also was."* Since we are going to face the same spirit, the prophecy in Timothy promises that God will reveal the folly in the same way. So now the question becomes a simple one: How was the folly manifested? The answer to that question emerges as we look at how God led Moses in preparation to face and ultimately vanquish the opposition. God was moving simultaneously on two fronts to fulfill His promises.

Genesis 15:13–16 tells us the length of time that the children of Israel were locked up in Egypt:

> Then He said to Abram: "Know certainly that your descendants will be strangers in a land that is not theirs, and will serve them, and they will afflict them four hundred years. And also the nation whom they serve I will judge; afterward they shall come out with great possessions. Now as for you, you shall go to your fathers in peace; you shall be buried at a good old age. But in the fourth generation they shall return here, for the iniquity of the Amorites is not yet complete."

At the end of four hundred years God covenanted with Abraham to bring the Jewish nation out of Egypt. The controlling factor was fullness of iniquity. Only after the owners of the promised land filled it with iniquity could they be dispossessed. The original possessor had not yet filled the land with iniquity, therefore they could not be removed. As the time of fulfillment approached, we see the preparation for the ministry of Moses expedited. Moses had to execute judgment on all the gods of Egypt. After these judgments, the nation would be released. The preparation took years. Persecution dramatically increased as they approached deliverance. The closer they came to the prophetic promise being realized, the greater the affliction and persecution that manifested. Exodus 1:12–14 says:

> But the more they afflicted them, the more they multiplied and grew. And they were in dread of the children of Israel. So the Egyptians made the children of Israel serve with rigor. And they made their lives bitter with hard bondage—in mortar, in brick, and in all manner of service in the field. All their service in which they made them serve was with rigor.

Fullness of iniquity was required in two arenas. The Egyptians had to fill the cup through their treatment of the Israelites, guaranteeing release after judgment on all their gods. The Cananites had to fill their land with iniquity to lose their ability to defend it. When iniquity is "full," the anointing to execute judgment comes. How many heads need to be cut off, how many innocent people need to be blown up, ***before we realize*** that radical Islam is filling a cup. Their stated goal is to dominate the entire world. Many Muslims refuse to condemn terrorists, revealing their true allegiance. If Muslim leaders fulfill their vows to develop nuclear weapons and obliterate Israel, the church loses the promised harvest of Romans 11. What choice does the church have except to execute spiritual judgment? When the purpose of the early church was threatened they responded. In Spiritual Boot Camp, we get acquainted with the God of war. We learn His ways so we can walk with Him in judgment, mercy, and faith. A Christian without faith for judgment is a warrior without a weapon!

Psalm 105:23–25 records God's hand behind the scenes filling the cup of iniquity so that judgment could come, releasing Israel:

> Israel also came into Egypt, And Jacob sojourned in the land of Ham. And He increased His people greatly, And made them stronger than their enemies. **He turned their heart to hate His people,** To deal craftily with His servants.

Why would God turn the heart of the Egyptian leadership *"to hate His people"* and to cause them great bitterness and bondage? The answer is because it filled the cup so that justice could be decreed, setting the people free. There is a parallel to what we face today with radical Islam. Jihadists as proponents of death, mayhem, and murder are filling a cup, and when judgment is executed their hold on Arab nations will be broken so these nations can hear the gospel. As a graduate of Officer Candidate School in the United States Navy, I can attest to the fact that our government does not send its military to war without necessary training. The first stage of that training, for me, consisted of Marine drill instructors, bloody knees, and a social status slightly lower than that of maggots. As tough as it was, when it was over, I had a different mentality concerning war and my participation in it. I wouldn't trade that experience for anything. Since abandoning the draft, we have two generations of Americans who are completely indifferent to the military and the preparation necessary to fight for the nation. Many of them have had their minds poisoned against our nation by their teachers and university professors! Thanks to "seeker sensitivity," many in the church have lost a warrior mentality!

Exodus 3:19–22 highlights God's pattern and purpose:

> But I am sure that the king of Egypt will not let you go, no, not
> even by a mighty hand. So I will stretch out My hand and strike
> Egypt with all My wonders which I will do in its midst; and after
> that he will let you go. And I will give this people favor in the sight
> of the Egyptians, and it shall be, when you go, that you shall not
> go empty–handed. But every woman shall ask of her neighbor,
> namely, of her who dwells near her house, articles of silver, articles
> of gold, and clothing; and you shall put them on your sons and
> on your daughters. So you shall plunder the Egyptians.

Righteous judgment dictated Egypt pay for their slave labor. Spoil
was executed as a judgment under the anointing given to Moses.
Exodus 2:23–25 portrays the "fullness" pattern!

> Now it happened in the process of time that the king of Egypt
> died. Then the children of Israel groaned because of the bondage,
> and they cried out; and their cry came up to God because of the
> bondage. So God heard their groaning, and God remembered
> His covenant with Abraham, with Isaac, and with Jacob. And
> God looked upon the children of Israel, and God acknowledged
> them.

James 5 promises God will acknowledge another group in the last
days. He will acknowledge the cries of his ministers for the funds
to fulfill their call and disciple nations. Like the children of Israel in
Egypt their cries initiate a promised prophetic financial judgment.
Deceived, demonized people have hoarded wealth for a season of
transfer. Isaiah saw this season and prophesied specific purposes of
financing the spread of the gospel.

There is a deep intercessory cry that only comes from agony
that is experienced in the natural. This intercessory cry has been
progressively rising all over the earth from Islamic brutality, Com-
munist persecution, and political pressure! Deep groans are rising.

The church is crying! God hears. He remembers His covenant, He acknowledges, and when He *"acknowledges,"* the anointing to execute the Word of the Lord comes! When Moses tried to bring God's promise to pass he met supernatural demonic resistance. When Paul and Barnabas were sent out from Antioch in Acts 13, they faced supernatural demonic resistance. What a blessing it would be if our Bible schools prepared ministers to execute the Didiche, as Paul did in Acts 13. After fifty years of neglecting Jesus the Judge, it is hard to find those who **know** Him. Jesus would say to us as leaders, *"You have neglected the weightier matters of the law, judgment, mercy, and faith."* It is not enough to teach "faith." It is not enough to teach "mercy." We have to bring the church to a place where their faith can minister mercy or minister judgment at the direction of the Holy Spirit. Until this level of training is achieved, we don't even have a platoon that we can send out to war as the early church did. Let the army of the Lord arise!

Paul prophesies to us who wind up the age, saying we will face the spirit of Jannes and Jambres, just as Moses did, in Second Timothy 3:8–9. Moses met supernatural resistance. Now the question is, Will we be prepared to do what Moses did when we face the spirit of Jannes and Jambres?

Exodus 7:10–13 chronicles the first encounter with Jannes and Jambres:

> So Moses and Aaron went in to Pharaoh, and they did so, just as the LORD commanded. And Aaron cast down his rod before Pharaoh and before his servants, and it became a serpent. But Pharaoh also called the wise men and the sorcerers; so the magicians of Egypt, they also did in like manner with their enchantments. For every man threw down his rod, and they became serpents. But Aaron's rod swallowed up their rods. And Pharaoh's heart grew hard, and he did not heed them, as the LORD had said.

The magicians were able to match what Moses did, supernaturally bringing forth the same kind of judgments. The first plague was blood in the waters. In verse 22 it says, *"Then the magicians of Egypt did so with their enchantments; and Pharaoh's heart grew hard, and he did not heed them, as the LORD had said."* The next plague was frogs, as mentioned in chapter 8, verses 1–2. In verse 7 we find, *"And the magicians did so with their enchantments, and brought up frogs on the land of Egypt."* The third plague was lice. Verse 18 of chapter 8 says, *"Now the magicians so worked with their enchantments to bring forth lice, **but they could not. . . .**"* In the spiritual war we are facing, demons can only emulate God to a point. In the third round they could no longer match Moses! And by the fifth round God was showing the difference between idol worshippers and true believers. The key phrase in Exodus 9 is the *"hand of the Lord."* Moses moved the hand of the Lord consistently until he brought about the deliverance promised. When Psalm 2 promises nations for an inheritance, how much judgment will be required to gain the promise? How many rounds of miracles will the enemy match until God demonstrates a difference? Are we ready for the battle ahead?

A church that cannot move the hand of God is a church that does not know its covenant. Because of the magnitude of the demonic power that we are going to face in these end–times, we have no choice but to jump into God's Boot Camp and learn how to walk in *"judgment, mercy and faith."* May the Army of the Lord arise!

Move into God's Boot Camp
Determined, whole-hearted
God's army arise now
Suit up & get started

Chapter 13

Ground School—The History of War

After Boot Camp, I started Ground School, where I learned aero-dynamics, aviation weather and the history of war. When you are graduating a warrior, it is essential to know the history of war, lest we repeat past mistakes. This is just as true in the spirit as it is in the natural. Psalm 149, in the first six verses, outlines a progression in praise and worship. But the last three verses end very uniquely, all beginning with the same word, "To . . . To . . . To. . . ." Verses 7–9 say what our worship should culminate in:

> To execute vengeance on the nations, And punishments on the peoples;
>
> To bind their kings with chains, And their nobles with fetters of iron;
>
> To execute on them the written judgment—This honor have all His saints.

The honor of this level of warfare in decreeing God's purposes by the Spirit certainly must have a history. A history that many of us, obviously, have missed because we see very few equipped to walk such a path. If we review the issue of "dominion" from its inception, in Genesis 1:26, perhaps this spiritual history will clearly emerge, giving us a background to understand the "*honor*" of which Psalm 149 speaks. Genesis 1:26 says:

> Then God said, "Let Us make man in Our image, according to Our likeness; let them have **dominion** over the fish of the sea, over the birds of the air, and over the cattle, over all the earth and over every creeping thing that creeps on the earth."

When God created man in His own image, His first act was to endow him with "dominion" over the creation. The problem was that man didn't keep it very long. In Genesis 3:6–7 we're told:

> So when the woman saw that the tree was good for food, that it was pleasant to the eyes, and a tree desirable to make one wise, she took of its fruit and ate. She also gave to her husband with her, and he ate. Then the eyes of both of them were opened, and they knew that they were naked; and they sewed fig leaves together and made themselves coverings.

Adam gave that "dominion" over to satan through disobedience. It is through covenantal obedience that God restores measures of that dominion to man. In Genesis 12:1–3 when God calls Abram He commands *"Get out of your country, From your kindred And from your father's house."* So Abram has to leave his country, his kindred and his culture. We find out why he has to leave his culture in Joshua 24:2 which says:

> And Joshua said to all the people, "Thus says the LORD God of Israel: 'Your fathers, including Terah, the father of Abraham and

the father of Nahor, dwelt on the other side of the river in old times; and they served other gods.'"

Obedience was required for deliverance from a culture of idolatry. This is true of every culture today, whether we are German, Asian, Hispanic, American, English, African or a multiple combination. Every culture has strengths. Those strengths are usually idolized by most of us who grew up in that culture. And God says if we are going to walk with Him we have to come out of our culture into His Kingdom culture. Kingdom culture is different from every other culture on the earth. In it, we think differently, the values are different, and we have to learn the **ways** of the Kingdom. In Kingdom culture, dominion can be covenantally accessed. The primary problem is the access point. We have to come into God's Throne with boldness and confidence! In Genesis 3:8, when God came looking for Adam and Eve the first thing they did was, *". . . hid themselves from the presence of the Lord God among the trees of the garden."* The reason why the covenant of "Sure Mercy" is so essential to moving up into the next level of our warfare is that it addresses this issue of hiding among the trees in guilt and shame. Communion with God is the product of a cleansed conscience. There is **only one** Name given under heaven by which a person's conscience can be free from guilt and shame—JESUS. His blood cleanses us from all sin!

In Isaiah 61:1–4 we are told:

The Spirit of the Lord God is upon Me, Because the Lord has anointed Me To preach good tidings to the poor; He has sent Me to heal the brokenhearted, To proclaim liberty to the captives, And the opening of the prison to those who are bound; To proclaim the acceptable year of the Lord, And the day of vengeance of our God; To comfort all who mourn, To console those who mourn in Zion, To give them beauty for ashes, The oil of joy for mourning,

The garment of praise for the spirit of heaviness; That they may be called **trees of righteousness**, The planting of the LORD, that He may be glorified.

The covenant of "Sure Mercy," while turning our failures into the platform for our greatest success, also transforms us from hiding among the trees to becoming a tree *"of righteousness, the planting of the LORD that He may be glorified."* Redeeming failure was not our idea. We were a failure going somewhere to happen which needed to be redeemed. God saw it before we ever got there and not only chose to redeem us but to make the place of our shame and source of hiding a place of confidence and us a *"tree of righteousness."* Only God can transform failure into a platform for success. How can we neglect such a great salvation?

Yielding to adultery and covering the pregnancy by murdering the husband became David's greatest failure, but for the rest of his life not only was he a tree of righteous in that same realm, but he was an extender of mercy everywhere he went. The yardstick of his life became a plumbline by which others were measured and judged. Who is sufficient for these things? God's covenant of mercy works! Our choice is to accept it, believe it, and act on it. Because it is only in cooperation with the Holy Spirit and confidence in the Throne Room that we can dispense dominion. Peter partnered with God to dispense dominion; the fruit was no sickness or disease could stand in his shadow. The same dominion that healed all, brought about the supernatural demise of Ananias and Sapphira. Dominion comes on God's terms, not on ours! The dominion of God has to be dispensed in the last days or we cannot obtain the nations that Jesus bought and paid for in His own death, burial and resurrection. Anything less is an insult to the blood of the Lamb!

In Psalm 2 we are told to ask for nations, because it is an inheritance, bought and paid for by Jesus Himself. Anything less dishonors

His sacrifice. When we attempt to disciple those nations, we will face demonic resistance. Demonic resistance has grown and organized to such a point that it threatens our nation. When Moses faced such equally intense enemies, he moved God's hand. God's judgment removed the obstacles. The early church was not oblivious to removing obstacles. Peter, through the Holy Spirit, announced to Ananias and Sapphira their eminent and immediate demise. Peter didn't flinch! Do we have a theology for moving the hand of God? Do we have a theology for executing the judgment written? Do we really believe it is an honor for the saints to participate with God? God believes it and declared it in His Word. Can we agree with Him?

When Jesus sent out the seventy, in Luke 10:19 He said this:

> Behold, I give you the authority to trample on serpents and scorpions, and over all the power of the enemy, and nothing shall by any means hurt you.

This level of authority and dominion was restored to the church in the Great Commission. In Matthew 28, Jesus said to us the exact thing He said to the seventy. Verses 18–20 state:

> Then Jesus came and spoke to them, saying, "All authority has been given to Me in heaven and on earth. Go therefore and make disciples of all the nations, baptizing them in the name of the Father and of the Son and of the Holy Spirit, teaching them to observe all things that I have commanded you; and lo, I am with you always, even to the end of the age."

The authority to remove the hindrances to the harvest has been bought and paid for by the Lord Jesus Christ. In the history of spiritual war, the examples are too numerous to deny. In Revelation 12:11 and 17 we are told:

And they overcame him by the blood of the Lamb and by the word of their testimony, and they did not love their lives to the death. . . . And the dragon was enraged with the woman, and he went to make war with the rest of her offspring, who keep the commandments of God and have the testimony of Jesus Christ.

We are in a war. Demons inspire people to come against the church and at this point in history they even move leaders of nations. Some national leaders seek nuclear weapons to destroy Israel and the U.S. Are we powerless in the face of such threats? Many leaders act as if we are. Spiritual history teaches us just the opposite. The first step in addressing this issue is becoming the *"trees of righteousness, the planting of the LORD."* Having confidence in the Throne Room is a product of having a heart free of guilt and shame. When our heart does not condemn us, we have confidence toward God. God wants warriors and the Word tells us that the end–time church will be an awesome warring army.

Joel 2:11 says:

The LORD gives voice before His army, For His camp is very great; For strong is the One who executes His word. For the day of the LORD is great and very terrible; Who can endure it?

If we back up to verses 5–10 we find out what this army of the LORD looks like that executes His Word:

With a noise like chariots over mountaintops they leap, Like the noise of a flaming fire that devours the stubble, Like a strong people set in battle array. Before them the people writhe in pain; All faces are drained of color, They run like mighty men, They climb the wall like men of war; Every one marches in formation, And they do not break ranks, They do not push one another;

Every one marches in his own column. And when they lunge between the weapons, They are not cut down. They run to and fro in the city, They run on the wall; They climb into the houses, They enter at the windows like a thief. The earth quakes before them, The heavens tremble; The sun and moon grow dark, And the stars diminish their brightness.

This army knows who they are. They are established in their purpose. They are mighty men. They are men of war. They march in formation. They do not break ranks. They have learned to submit one to the other. They do not push one another. They do not offend one another. They do not try to step in each other's space. They march in their own column and they cannot be stopped! They cannot be cut down! They are not diminished by their losses! Even the creation begins to quake before them as they demand the Word of the Lord in manifestation. It is time to graduate from Ground School.

Are we that awesome warring army
Out of Boot Camp . . . in the fray
Wielding mercy's sword of judgment
Clothed with confidence today?

Chapter 14

Elementary Flight Training

The next stage of training for me began at Saufley Field in Pensacola, Florida, where I began Elementary Flight Training. We not only had to learn the peculiarities of our aircraft, but why specific things had to be done in a specific order. The order was so important that checklists were created to insure nothing was omitted.

Elementary Flight Training for believers in this season has very specific goals. Understanding the three different barriers that God erected to stop people from losing their land is essential. When these three barriers are dissolved, any people group forfeits their ability to defend their land. At this point, the country can be lost unless we use the covenant of "Sure Mercy" to stop the judgment long enough to gain a harvest. Stopping the judgment may demand dealing with the offending agents. The examples we have from Moses' life restore the nation by bringing justice to the polluting, defiling, offending parties. In God's love and care for people and nations, He sets three primary barriers which have to be breached before national sovereignty can be lost.

John 8:4–9 shows us the first barrier against losing a nation. It says:

"Teacher, this woman was caught in adultery, in the very act. Now Moses, in the law, commanded us that such should be stoned. But what do You say?" This they said, testing Him, that they might have something of which to accuse Him. But Jesus stooped down and wrote on the ground with His finger, as though He did not hear. So when they continued asking Him, He raised Himself up and said to them, "He who is without sin among you, let him throw a stone at her first." And again He stooped down and wrote on the ground. Then those who heard it, being convicted by their conscience, went out one by one, beginning with the oldest even to the last. And Jesus was left alone, and the woman standing in the midst.

Jesus appealed to conscience. Verse 9 tells us, *"Then those who heard it, being convicted by their conscience, went out one by one. . . ."* Individual conscience is the very first barrier against losing a nation. Our individual conscience witnesses about good and evil. People can choose sin continually until their conscience is seared and no longer registers an opposing voice. At this point, their only hope resides in barriers two and three.

The second barrier God established to make people uncomfortable after searing their own conscience is in Leviticus 20:22–23:

You shall therefore keep all **My statutes** and all **My judgments**, and perform them, that the land where I am bringing you to dwell may not vomit you out. And you shall not walk in the **statutes** of the nation which I am casting out before you; for they commit all these things, and therefore I abhor them.

Our forefathers placed a barrier to loss of the land in our country with the laws they passed because **laws express corporate or national conscience**. Our laws express the conscience of our culture. An individual conscience can be seared relatively quickly; it takes longer to defile the corporate conscience. Sodomy laws lasted two hundred years in America. Our forefathers were wise enough to legislate from a Kingdom culture. Legislating from a Kingdom culture discriminates against sin so that God does not judge the nation. As long as we legally discriminated against abortion and homosexuality, the nation was blessed. As the national conscience has become progressively defiled and barriers removed, America's plight has grown correspondingly more desperate. As rapidly as possible, the radical homosexual and lesbian networks are working to remove all corporate laws that express biblical conscience. *No nation in history has ever survived opening the floodgate of statutorial protection for perversion.* Rome quickly descended into devastation and destruction. **When the land fills with iniquity, judgment comes!** Judgment brought the end of Israel as a nation. Our future is filled with devastating national judgments if this permissive perilous path persists!

Romans 1 outlines a seven-step slide into loss of national conscience resulting in the ultimate judgment—loss of the nation. Romans 1:18–20 says:

> For the wrath of God revealed from heaven against all ungodliness and unrighteousness of men, who suppress the truth in unrighteousness, because what may be known of God is manifest in them, for God has shown it to them.

We are without excuse because God has revealed Himself in the creation. In step one of this descent, verse 21a says, *"Because, although they knew God, they did not glorify Him as God."* A good example of this would be the 1972 Supreme Court decision to remove prayer from public schools. It is a perfect example of a nation that *"knew God, but did not glorify Him as God."* The second test in verse 21 is *"nor were thankful."* The Supreme Court decrees disallowing any display of manger scenes from any public grounds, including schools during Christmas time is an example of what fulfills number two. The third step from the same verse says, *"but became futile in their thoughts."* An example of the futility in thinking of court decisions is the removal of the Ten Commandments, which is known as the very foundation of all moral governmental law in western civilization. How could we have come to a season where our fathers inscribed these Ten Commandments on our public buildings but we can no longer use them publicly?

Step four says, *"and their foolish hearts were darkened."* Roe v. Wade was the decision that fully manifested this fourth step. When the most innocent among us can be murdered at will, we are on our way to **losing a national conscience concerning evil**. Number five is found in verse 22, *"Professing to be wise, they became fools."* The classic example of this would be the embracing of secular humanism in our school system to *replace* biblical morality. The sixth example in this descent into the loss of national conscience is in verse 23. It says, *"and changed the glory of the incorruptible God into an image made like corruptible man—and birds and four-footed beasts and creeping things."* The proliferation of nature worship in giving animals "rights" and consequently taking them away from man makes man now *subservient to the animals* rather than the animals under the **dominion** of man. Man's dominion has been taken away by the animal rights movement. This amounts to nature worship! God did not give animals dominion over man. He gave man dominion over animals. Anytime you give animals "rights," you have to take those "rights" away from man. It is an abomination!

The animal rights movement, along with the radical environmental movement, is a manifestation of nature worship that is **destroying national conscience** and opening the door to devastation and destruction. *21st Century Science & Technology Magazine* estimates the 1972 banning of DDT has cost sixty million needless deaths.

Professor Emeritus J. Gordon Edwards at San Jose State University "drank a spoonful of DDT in front of his entomology classes at the beginning of each school year, to make the point that DDT is not harmful to human beings. Now 83, and still fighting for the truth about DDT, Edwards is an avid mountain climber."[3] Banning DDT through junk science offers up in sacrifice the elderly and innocent at the altar of nature worship. Sacrificing man to protect mosquitoes makes nature an idol! Mosquito worshippers are winning in offering humanity up to malaria, West Nile virus, and dengue fever for the sake of environmental purity. Another example of this idolatry is seen in the multiple variety of lawsuits against logging in the west where overpopulation and density of trees has opened the door to the bark beetle and unstoppable devastating wild fires. We can thank the environmentalists for exacerbating major wild fires and creating devastation in western forests by fighting for density. Every lawsuit to stop logging promotes the fire hazard. After three years fighting wild land fires and almost losing his life, a member of our family shared about the devastating impact of the demonized dominating environmental community.

The seventh and final step where God is justified in giving the land to others is in Romans 1:24–32 where national leadership approves and promotes homosexuality and lesbianism. No nation can withstand statutorily approving and protecting homosexuality and lesbianism and yet there has been a steady progression of it through our courts. Worshipping the creature rather than the Creator has always been the core of idolatry. In Paul's day, it started with meat sacrificed to idols and culminated in temple prostitution. Today's idolatry continues its sexual expression in homosexuality, lesbianism and pornography. President Bill Clinton had the distinction of

---

3 Marjorie Mazel Hecht "Bring Back DDT, and Science With it!" *21st Century Science & Technology Magazine,* Editorial Summer 2002.

pushing America past the seventh and final step of this descent into destruction. In the first week in office the Clinton administration moved to legalize homosexuality in the military! It was during the early Clinton years that while on an airplane bound for an Intercession for the Nations Conference, the voice of the Lord came to me saying, **"An outcry has come to Me against your nation!"**

Thank God there is one other barrier to the loss of sovereignty as a nation. Can we count on it to hold back the tide while we battle the deceiving spirits of darkness? First Timothy 4:1–3 says:

> Now the Spirit expressly says that in latter times some will depart from the faith, giving heed to deceiving spirits and doctrines of demons, speaking lies in hypocrisy, having their own conscience seared with a hot iron, forbidding to marry, and commanding to abstain from foods which God created to be received with thanksgiving by those who believe and know the truth.

We are seeing the fruit of many a *"seared conscience"* on the national level. That should prove the necessity of learning how to fly so we can execute the judgment written in order to stop destruction and recover a harvest from the nation!

The corporate national conscience reflected in our laws is under assault. Men and women whose conscience has been seared with a hot iron have dedicated their lives to destroying the national conscience. This path uninterrupted ends in ever–increasing national judgment, destruction . . . and death. There has never been a greater assault on marriage between a man and a woman than there is right now! Let's learn to fly this plane so we can deliver some ordinance, arrest the enemies advances and stop the devastation—long enough for a harvest.

Even if the national conscience gets seared, God still provides a third and final voice of conscience in a land in order that they might turn and not be lost or destroyed. Isaiah 59:17–19 says:

> For He put on righteousness as a breastplate, And a helmet of salvation on His head; He put on the garments of vengeance for clothing, And was clad with zeal as a cloak. According to their deeds, accordingly He will repay, Fury to His adversaries, Recompense to His enemies; The coastlands He will fully repay. So shall they fear The name of the LORD from the west, And His glory from the rising of the sun; When the enemy comes in like a flood, The Spirit of the LORD will lift up a standard against him.

Jesus, in anointing the church, has promised that when *"the enemy comes in like a flood, The Spirit of the LORD will lift up a standard against him."* That standard is the church! That standard is the corporate anointing that is birthed by a remnant of people who choose to walk out God's Word. The church has a voice. The church has an obligation to take their voice and declare the Word of the Lord to their generation. In America the only thing that stands between the loss of our nation, because of the seven–step slide being complete, is the church! The prophetic spirit in the church is our lone remaining barrier! Who is willing to speak the truth to the land and to our leaders saying, "You cannot do this. If you allow homosexual marriage you fill the land with iniquity and you bring increasing adversity and ever greater judgments upon us." No nation can withstand a baptism of perversion like Sodom and Gomorrah!

The problem with the church is that we have denominations now that are choosing to ordain homosexual bishops, so there are sections of the church that are turning apostate. When a believer supports a national organization with their giving that has chosen to ordain homosexuals, they open their family to that perversion and line themselves up for covenant judgment! Wisdom dictates we flee the wrath to come! Those sections of the church need to dry up and blow away! The last hope of any nation is the church! **If the church accepts sin and compromises with the culture then the church contributes to the destruction of the land and loss of the nation. God deliver us!**

If we treat sin with compromise
Then we have broken covenant ties

Concerning evil . . . Shrinking back
Will boot us off our calling's track

May we train well to fly to heights
Where holy power with awe ignites

Chapter 15

Intermediate Flight Training

I will never forget the first time I walked out on the flight line at Whiting Field near Milton, Florida. I looked at the T28 Trojan, an aircraft that was used for close air support early in the Vietnam campaign. Many of the planes still had bomb racks. It held the climb record to five thousand feet for a short time with a massive radial engine, and giant three–bladed prop generating fifty-six inches of manifold air pressure for maximum take–off power. You could raise the gear and the flaps and by the time you got to the end of a long runway you could crank it straight up to nearly five thousand feet before having to level off. It is the only airplane I ever flew with a speed brake and the one we used to learn formation flying and air combat. There are times when you know that you have graduated into a whole different realm of warfare, just by the equipment that you are flying. There is a parallel in the realm of the Spirit based on revelation of God's Word.

Isaiah 55 has such a transition in the promise of the covenant of "Sure Mercy." Verses 3–7 state:

> Incline your ear, and come to Me. Hear, and your soul shall live;
> And I will make an everlasting covenant with you—the sure mer-

cies of David. Indeed I have given him as a witness to the people. A leader and commander for the people. Surely you shall call a nation you do not know, And nations who do not know you shall run to you, Because of the Lord your God, And the Holy One of Israel; For He has glorified you. Seek the Lord while He may be found, Call upon Him while He is near. Let the wicked forsake his way, And the unrighteous man his thoughts; Let him return to the Lord, And He will have mercy on him; And to our God, For He will abundantly pardon.

Within the promise of the covenant of "Sure Mercy" emerges an exhortation to return to the Lord, obtain mercy so that we can be a dispenser of the covenant. Confidence is essential in the Throne Room and the transition comes in verses 8–11 which say:

"For My thoughts are not your thoughts, Nor are your ways My ways," says the Lord. "For as the heavens are higher than the earth, So are My ways higher than your ways, And My thoughts than your thoughts. For as the rain comes down, and the snow from heaven, And do not return there, But water the earth, And make it bring forth and bud, That it may give seed to the sower And bread to the eater, So shall My word be that goes forth from My mouth; It shall not return to Me void, But it shall accomplish what I please, And it shall prosper in the thing for which I sent it."

The promise of the covenant of "Sure Mercy" is that when we put it in our mouth and we return it to the Lord it will not return void, but it will accomplish what He pleases and will prosper in the thing for which He sent it! Operating in this realm is like transitioning into a new aircraft. Sometimes we spend years looking at scriptural promises through the eyes of our tradition and when that happens our tradition hides what God is trying to reveal, and suddenly He has to open our eyes so that we see it. This happened to me in studying the covenant of "Sure Mercy." In Second Samuel 7, where Nathan extends the covenant of "Sure Mercy" to David, for five years I read over verses 8 and 9 and missed the second edge of the sword. The first edge of the sword we use to silence the accuser of the brethren. We must accept redemption for our failures as a platform for moving into covenant fulfillment. The second edge of the sword here deals with the actual enemies who rise up under demonic influence to hinder or completely stop God's purposes. Verses 8–9 say:

> Now therefore, thus shall you say to My servant David, "Thus says the LORD of hosts: 'I took you from the sheepfold, from following the sheep, to be ruler over My people, over Israel. And I have been with you wherever you have gone, and have **cut off** all your enemies from before you, and have made you a great name, like the name of the great men who are on the earth.'"

God said to David, *"I have been with you wherever you have gone, and have **cut off** all your enemies from before you."* The Hebrew word for "cut off" is **kaw-rath. Kaw-rath** generally means to "cut off or cut away." The first appearance of **kaw-rath** in Scripture is Genesis 9:11 where we are told, *"Thus I establish My covenant with you: Never again shall all flesh be **cut off** by the waters of the flood; never again shall there be a flood to destroy the earth."*

God promises not to **kaw-rath** His own people!

The second appearance is in Genesis 15 where it is used for the cutting of the covenant. Verse 18 says, *"On the same day the LORD made [**kaw-rath**] a covenant with Abram, saying. . . ."* Whenever a blood covenant was made it always had to be "cut" and the word that is used generally is **kaw-rath**. The word for *"covenant"* is **ber-eeth**. Verse 18 says, *"On the same day the LORD made a covenant [**ber-eeth**]. . . ."* Sometimes God uses the word **kaw-rath** when He means **ber-eeth,** demonstrating that the covenant defines mercy to David as destruction to the enemy. One of the primary ways God manifests mercy to David is by destroying, removing and cutting off the enemy so they are no longer hindering David's God–appointed purpose. Therefore, David has the responsibility of invoking the covenant of mercy over his life and it's up to God to "cut off" the enemy. Mercy to David, or mercy to Israel, means "cutting off" the enemy. Covenant mercy does not necessarily mean the transformation of enemies, but it does mean the removal of their resistance. Over and over again we find that David is a man of war! In Acts 13 we are also told he is a man after God's own heart. To understand David and the covenant of mercy is to understand God's heart for war and His willingness to deal with our enemies.

The Treasury of Scripture Knowledge[4] says of Psalm 143, "The LXX., Volgate, Ethopic, and Arabic state that this Psalm was composed by David on the rebellion of his son Absalom." Psalm 143 is a perfect example of David invoking his covenant of "Sure Mercy" in a season of war where the loss of office was a reality. The fruit of invoking this covenant was destruction of the enemy. The problem was that the enemy was within David's family. At least he realized the necessity of asking God not to enter into judgment with him in verses 1–2:

> Hear my prayer, O Lord, Give ear to my supplications! In Your faithfulness answer me, And in Your righteousness. Do not enter into judgment with Your servant, For in Your sight no one living is righteous.

David was in need of mercy. He was asking for it and asking for God

---

4   *The Treasury of Scripture Knowledge: Five Hundred Thousand Scripture References and parallel Passages.* Oak Harbor: Logos Research Systems, Inc. 1995.

to deal with his enemies. But verse 12 encapsulates David's view of the covenant of "Sure Mercy." He prayed, *"In Your mercy **cut off** my enemies, And destroy all those who afflict my soul; For I am Your servant."* Covenant mercy to David meant the absolute removal of his enemy. He was asking God to put an end to the captivity that the enemy had perpetrated on his life and for the nation. David understood the warfare side of the covenant of "Sure Mercy." He understood there was a second edge to this sword and he had no hesitation in executing the judgment written.

The Second Chronicles 7:14 movement encouraging prayer for the nation had this element hidden in the passage. If we had looked beyond verse 14 into the context of the passage, we would have discovered God's invitation to enter a whole new dimension of warfare by invoking the covenant of "Sure Mercy"! Verse 14 says:

> If My people who are called by My name will humble themselves, and pray and seek My face, and turn from their wicked ways, then I will hear from heaven, and will forgive their sin and heal their land.

We focused on verse 14 assuming identificational repentance would satisfy all requirements but the next few verses exhort us toward imprecatory mercy. Verses 15–18 say:

> Now My eyes will be open and My ears attentive to prayer made in this place. For now I have chosen and sanctified this house, that My name may be there forever; and My eyes and My heart will be there perpetually. As for you, if you walk before Me as your father David walked, and do according to all that I have commanded you, and if you keep My statutes and My judgments, then I will establish the throne of your kingdom, as I **covenanted** with David your father, saying, "You shall never fail to have a man as ruler in Israel."

In verse 18 when God says, *"I will establish the throne of your kingdom, as I **covenanted** with David your father,"* we would think normally that the Hebrew word **ber-eeth** would have been used. However, God did not use **ber-eeth**, but He used **kaw-rath**. In effect what He said is, *"I will establish the throne of your kingdom, as I cut* [meaning the covenant] *with David your father, saying 'You shall never fail to have a man as ruler in Israel.'"*

Perhaps there are other places where God uses **kaw-rath** for covenant. In Haggai 2:4–5 we find:

> "Yet now be strong, Zerubbabel," says the LORD; "and be strong, Joshua, son of Jehozadak, the high priest; and be strong, all you people of the land," says the LORD, "and work; for I am with you," says the LORD of hosts. " According to the word that I **covenanted** [**kaw-rath**] with you when you came out of Egypt, so My Spirit remains among you; do not fear!"

God refers to the word He gave them when He brought them out of Egypt as His covenant, using the word **kaw-rath**, to mean the cutting of the covenant. This tells us that when God gives us a prophetic word, He is cutting a covenant with us to manifest that word. We could just as easily translate Second Samuel 7:9, *"And I have been with you wherever you have gone, and have covenanted all your enemies from before you."* We could go back to a number of places where David in the Psalms is invoking his covenant of mercy simultaneously asking God to cut off the enemy. The real question is, How did David view his covenant of "Sure Mercy"? The answer to that is in the Psalms he wrote. In Psalm 3:5–8 we are told:

> I lay down and slept, I awoke, for the LORD sustained me; I will not be afraid of ten thousands of people Who have set themselves against me all around. Arise, O LORD; Save me, O my God! For

You have struck all my enemies on the cheekbone; You have broken the teeth of the ungodly. Salvation belongs to the LORD, Your blessing is upon Your people. Selah.

In David's mind, salvation came when in God's mercy He *"struck all his enemies on the cheekbone."* In Psalm 12:1–3:

Help, LORD, for the godly man ceases! For the faithful disappear from among the sons of men. They speak idly everyone with his neighbor; With flattering lips and a double heart they speak. May the LORD **cut off** all flattering lips, And the tongue that speaks proud things.

David asked the LORD to *". . . cut off* [**kaw-rath**] *remove . . . all flattering lips . . . and a tongue that speaks proud things, and over the enemy who says 'we will prevail.'"* When it comes to war, David understands that covenant mercy to him means God's sword upon the enemy.

In Psalm 37 David gets on a roll with declaring the covenanting of his enemies. In verse 9 he says, *"For evildoers shall be* [covenanted] ***cut off****; But those who wait on the LORD, They shall inherit the earth."* In verse 22 he says, *"For those who are blessed by Him shall inherit the earth, But those who are cursed by Him shall be* [**kaw-rath**] *. . . cut off."* In verse 28 he says, *"For the LORD loves justice, And does not forsake His saints; They are preserved forever, But the descendants of the wicked shall be cut off* [**kaw-rath**—covenanted]. *"* Verse 34 says, *"Wait on the LORD, And keep His way, And He shall exalt you to inherit the land; When the wicked are* [**kaw-rath**] *cut off, you shall see it."* Finally verse 38 says, *"But the transgressors shall be destroyed together; The future of the wicked shall be* [**kaw-rath**] *cut off."*

Mercy for David means the "cutting off" of the enemy. He has no hesitation in praying it, in declaring it, or in decreeing it. David's prayers in the Psalms reflect the warrior's heart and his covenant of "Sure Mercy." Concerning Psalm 55:8, *"I would hasten my escape from the windy storm and tempest,"* The Treasury Of Scripture Knowledge comments that this refers to Absalom and his rebellious party. Verses 12–16 state:

> For it is not an enemy who reproaches me; Then I could bear it. Nor is it one who hates me who has magnified himself against me; Then I could hide from him. But it was you, a man my equal, My companion and my acquaintance. We took sweet counsel together, And walked to the house of God in the throng. **Let death seize them** [man after God's own heart]; Let them go down alive into hell, For wickedness is in their dwellings and among them. As for me, I will call upon God, And the LORD shall save me.

Mercy to David meant judgment to the enemy. He continually invoked his covenant of "Sure Mercy" and just as God promised; He "cut off" all of David's enemies. The interesting question is, how strong is this covenant of "Sure Mercy" when it is invoked over an enemy? The answer to that, of course, comes in the context of Psalm 143 where David, on the way out of Jerusalem, invokes his covenant of mercy over the enemy and the enemy just happens to be his own son, Absalom. He says in verse 12, *"In Your mercy **cut off** my enemies, And **destroy** all those who afflict my soul; For I am Your servant."* David appealed to God to perform covenant.

In Second Samuel 18:5 David commanded the three leaders of the different sections of his army saying, *"Now the king had commanded Joab, Abishai, and Ittai, saying 'Deal gently for my sake with the young man Absalom,' And all the people heard when the king gave all the captains orders concerning Absalom."* In the next few verses Absalom meets David's army and his hair gets caught in a terebinth tree where he hangs above the ground. A soldier sees it and reports it to Joab. Verses 11–14 state:

> So Joab said to the man who told him, "You just saw him! And

why did you not strike him there to the ground? I would have given you ten shekels of silver and a belt." But the man said to Joab, "Though I were to receive a thousand shekels of silver in my hand, I would not raise my hand against the king's son. For in our hearing the king commanded you and Abishai and Ittai, saying, 'Beware lest anyone touch the young man Absalom! Otherwise I would have dealt falsely against my own life. For there is nothing hidden from the king, and you yourself would have set yourself against me.' Then Joab said, "I cannot linger with you." And he took three spears in his hand and thrust them through Absalom's heart, while he was still alive in the midst of the terebinth tree.

Isn't it interesting that Joab is faced with the king's command not to touch Absalom and yet the covenant of "Sure Mercy" that David invoked now finds a leader who will take three spears, possibly one each for the Father, Son, and Holy Spirit (covenant makers), and throws them into Absalom's heart? Even though David commanded the army not to touch Absalom, the covenant of "Sure Mercy" he invoked brought exactly what he prayed on the enemy. And his own commands to his own army could not stop the covenant once invoked! How strong is the covenant of "Sure Mercy"? It takes someone stopping the rotation of the sun in order to grind it to a halt. The question is, will we ever grow to the place where we, like David, are believers after God's own heart and can invoke the covenant of "Sure Mercy," expecting God to do for us what He did for David? A good intercessory session can produce all the thrills of a bombing run, especially when the demonic structure holding men and women captive is dramatically damaged.

Transitioning to walk in truth
With this level of power
May the Spirit guide us, Lord
With wisdom in this hour!

Chapter 16

Carrier Qualification

I had so much fun flying the T28 Trojan that I had almost forgotten an occasional appendage on a few of the planes. It was a black and white striped pole called a "tail hook." The time came when we learned a different definition for "meatball." The next phase was all about learning how to fly that "meatball" all the way into the deck, cutting the engine at the Landing Signal Officer's (LSO) command. I had so many controlled crashes that I thought I was going to need dental work. When the LSO said, "Okay, you're all ready," we flew out to the Lexington at an altitude of five thousand feet. At five thousand feet that carrier looked like a dime on the ground and I thought, "How in the world am I ever going to get this plane on deck?" But after descending down to pattern altitude of one thousand feet, it looked just big enough to take a shot. When stress is overwhelming, we return to doing what has been learned in training by rote repetition! When it comes to flying, there is nothing quite like putting your airplane on a carrier deck! It is a pinnacle experience!

Oftentimes in the realm of the Spirit, it is hard to get through barriers that are erected by our tradition and theology. After one hundred years of pastoral and evangelistic messages dominating pulpits, the church is much more adept at salvation and personal care than Davidic warfare. The demonic doctrine of cultural tolerance practiced by seeker–sensitive Christianity is like a deadly serpent's venom robbing the church of its salt! "Turn the other cheek" Christianity is so dominant we have lost our admonition to be Bereans. Second Timothy 2:15 says, *"Be diligent to present yourself approved to God, a worker who does not need to be ashamed, rightly dividing the word of truth."* The church is very lopsided in emphasis. Jesus taught Kingdom where the presence of the King ruled over everything, including demonized leaders. The reason why we are told to study and divide the word of truth is because "truth" is held in tension. Western thinking always says, "It is either one way or the other; it has to be concrete." But that is not necessarily true in Hebrew thinking. In Hebrew thinking "truth" can be held in tension. An example of "truth being held in tension" in Peter's life would start in First Peter 2:20–24 where he exhorts us:

> For what credit is it if, when you are beaten for your faults, you take it patiently? But when you do good and suffer for it, if you take it patiently, this is commendable before God. For to this you were called, because Christ also suffered for us, leaving us an example, that you should follow His steps: "Who committed no sin, Nor was guile found in His mouth;" who, when He was reviled, did not revile in return; when He suffered, He did not threaten, but committed Himself to Him who judges righteously; for Himself bore our sins in His own body on the tree, that we, having died to sins, might live for righteousness—by whose stripes you were healed.

If we neglect to balance this passage with Acts, Romans and Revelation, then the fruit would look like the passivity of the American church. Peter is telling us how to operate in a social context when we want to win people to the Lord. He tells us that Jesus was our example and that *". . . when He was reviled He did not revile in return, when He suffered He did not threaten but committed Himself to the one who judges righteously."* That is true of Jesus in the gospels. When Jesus ascended and was seated at the right hand of God, He no longer turned the other cheek because he entered spiritual government. In the book of Revelation, speaking to the seven churches, He becomes the Judge of all the earth! He stills the storm in the gospels. In Revelation 2 He says, "If you don't repent I will send a storm." He becomes the Judge. The same Peter who wrote First Peter 2 also in Acts 5 stood up and announced the death of Ananias and Sapphira governmentally. Peter would never have written what is in First Peter 2 if he thought there was a conflict between what he said about how we conduct our lives versus what he did in a position of church government! How we conduct our lives in the social environment in which we live does not excuse us from governmental responsibility, whether it be political or spiritual.

Revelation 1 declares we have been made kings and priests unto our God. Kings execute judgment. Priests intercede for sinners bringing salvation. As the church we have said "yes" to priestly ministry and "no" to kingly ministry. Romans 13 declares God's call upon government to bear the sword. Romans 12–13 present both truths in tension. In Romans 12:14 Paul says, *"Bless those who persecute you; bless and do not curse."* The Greek word for curse here means to execute or imprecate doom. The rest of the chapter amplifies this application socially but immediately in chapter 13 Paul draws the distinction between a Christian's social behavior and governmental behavior. Romans 13:1–4 states:

> Let every soul be subject to the governing authorities. For there is no authority except from God, and the authorities that exist are appointed by God. Therefore whoever resists the authority resists

the ordinance of God, and those who resist will bring judgment on themselves. For rulers are not a terror to good works, but to evil. Do you want to be unafraid of the authority? Do what is good, and you will have praise from the same. For he is God's minister to you for good. But if you do evil, be afraid; for he does not bear the sword in vain; for he is God's minister, an avenger to execute wrath on him who practices evil.

If we are God's ministers, then we must bear the spiritual sword. Many ministers have parked their spiritual swords in the attic. Spiritual swords proclaim the judgment written so God can perform it! Spiritual government decrees the sword, executing wrath on those practicing evil.

Being a spiritual king speaks of governmental authority as God's minister charged with the responsibility of executing wrath or judgment. In Peter's governmental position in Acts 5, he had to execute God's judgment on Ananias and Sapphira. The prohibitions that applied socially, did not apply governmentally.

Paul says in Romans 12:19–20:

Beloved, do not avenge yourselves, but rather give place to wrath; for it is written, "Vengeance is Mine, I will repay," says the Lord. Therefore if your enemy hungers, feed him; If he thirsts, give him a drink; For in so doing you will heap coals of fire on his head.

In Acts 13:8 Paul met an enemy named Elymas the sorcerer. For some strange reason, he neither fed him nor gave him drink as advised in Romans 12. The social admonitions did not apply in a governmental situation. Paul executed the judgment of blindness as a doctrine of the Lord. The Lord's doctrines are the same *"yesterday, today and forever."*

Jesus held these same truths in the same tension in Matthew's gospel. In chapter 5, verse 44, He said, *"But I say to you, love your enemies, bless those who curse you, do good to those who hate you, and pray for those who spitefully use you and persecute you."* But in chapter 21, verses 19–21a, He said:

And seeing a fig tree by the road, he came to it and found nothing on it but leaves, and said to it. "Let no fruit grow on you ever again." And immediately the fig tree withered away. Now when the disciples saw it, they marveled, saying, "How did the fig tree wither away so soon?" So Jesus answered and said to them, "Assuredly, I say to you, if you have faith and do not doubt, you will not only do what was done to the fig tree. . . ."

Mark's version specifically says Jesus cursed the fig tree and Jesus specifically said if we had faith and did not doubt we would do the same. The context is in cleansing the national temple from the defiling corruption of mammon. To sum up Jesus' teaching in Matthew: in social settings, no imprecatory proclamations are needed but as a king in governmental situations we will be led to do as He did. Jesus said we would curse fig trees and they would wither away never to defile the ground again! Jesus cleansed the temple twice. First at the beginning of His ministry in John 2 and at the end of His ministry in Mark 11. Cleansing the temple should start at church and move to every branch of government. Let the cleansing begin!

Romans 13:3–4 state:

For rulers are not a **terror** to good works, but to evil. Do you want to be unafraid of the authority? Do what is good, and you will have praise from the same. For he is God's minister to you for good. But if you do evil, be afraid; for he does not **bear the sword in vain**; for he is God's minister, an avenger to execute wrath on him who practices evil.

Both spiritual and political governments bear the sword for God to execute wrath on evil doers. The best dictionary of the Bible is the Bible. The best definition of Bible terms is in the Bible. When we ask ourselves what the Bible means when it says *"bear the sword,"* all we have to do is go to First Samuel 15:8 and look at the context in which God commands Saul to destroy the Amalekites. Verse 8 says, *"He also took Agag king of the Amalekites alive, and utterly destroyed all the people with the edge of the sword."* The Bible definition of *"bearing the sword"* for political government is killing those who choose evil! Executing wrath is a function of government—political and spiritual. When we send a soldier off to war to minister God's wrath, we do not expect him to turn the other cheek to the enemy. We send soldiers to war and we expect them to kill the enemy. There is no conflict in conduct between these two positions. Those in spiritual leadership are expected to manage the government of God, just as those in political leadership have to send our troops off to war as a minister for God. Bearing the spiritual sword means decreeing God's Word over the enemy! The church can no longer only function socially and still keep our nation. We must now function governmentally to stop the enemy so we can have a harvest! It is time to take the promises of God and put this airplane on the carrier deck in the middle of the ocean—*because we are in a war.* Wayward untouchable Supreme Court justices are not "untouchable" for God. Wars are not won socially. They are won governmentally! Settle the issue! Land the plane! Take your place in spiritual government! Learn to proclaim the "judgment written" ***NOW!!!***

Let's function governmentally
Move forth . . . Arrest our enemy
If we turn cheeks . . . to keep our land
We'll lose our course like sinking sand

Chapter 17

Advanced Flight Training

I had to leave Florida and move to South Texas for the next stage of training. The place was Corpus Christi, Texas, and I was finally entering Advanced Flight Training, transitioning from single–engine to multi–engine. The only problem with the multi–engine training plane was that the wings folded—hopefully only on the ground. Flying an airplane with wings that fold does not inspire confidence when in the air. None of the trainers had air–conditioning. Every flight was a guaranteed five percent weight loss. In addition to the joy of flying a machine that was extremely suspect, I endured one of the worst hurricanes ever to come through Corpus Christi. It blew the roof off the barracks and dramatically damaged the Bachelor Officer Quarters. At the end of it, I walked out as a LTjg with a set of gold Navy wings—one step closer to combat! When you get to Advanced Flight Training, the realization dawns that you've mastered the basics and know how to fly, but now you are adding the skills that will one day give access to the most advanced technology in offense and defense that your nation offers.

Growth in the Spirit is amazingly parallel. There are things that God cannot trust us with when our character or judgment does not match the maneuvers we want to make. In many ways warfare in the spirit has the same critical issue! When character and charisma meet, business gets done in the Throne Room. The covenant of "Sure Mercy" was given to David but the times in which he lived were, in fact, unique. David knew the cost of a corrupt priesthood. He experienced it during his youth. He was anointed for ministry by Samuel. Samuel grew up in the midst of monumental manipulation. The sins of Eli were so bad people hated going to church and abhorred the offering. Corruption in the priesthood forfeited covenantal judgment allowing the Philistines to plunder Israel at will. History often repeats itself.

First Samuel 7 outlines the difference and shows what character produces in relationship with God. First Samuel 7:7–10 says:

> Now when the Philistines heard that the children of Israel had gathered together at Mizpah, the lords of the Philistines went up against Israel. And when the children of Israel heard of it, they were afraid of the Philistines. So the children of Israel said to Samuel, "Do not cease to cry out to the LORD our God for us, that He may save us from the hand of the Philistines." And Samuel took a suckling lamb and offered it as a whole burnt offering to the LORD. Then Samuel cried out to the LORD for Israel, and the LORD answered him. Now as Samuel was offering up the burnt offering, the Philistines drew near to battle against Israel. But the LORD thundered with a loud thunder upon the Philistines that day, and so confused them that they were overcome before Israel.

When Samuel prayed, the Philistines were routed. This was **not so** with his predecessors. First Samuel 7:15 indicates the position in which Samuel walked. Samuel was a judge in Israel. The Hebrew word for "judge" is **shaw-fat.** When a **shaw-fat,** or judge, issued a decree or spoke a prophetic word, that prophetic word became a **mish-pawt**. A **mish-pawt** was a judgment. It is **impossible** to have justice without judgment. Samuel maintained a pure priesthood. The power of that pure priesthood, or the fruit of it, is seen in First Samuel 7:13. *"So the Philistines were **subdued,** and they did not come anymore into the territory of Israel. And the **hand of the L**ORD *was against the Philistines all the days of Samuel."* Samuel conducted his priesthood in such a way that when he prayed, God's hand moved! Unfortunately, that was not the fruit of Eli, the previous priest. In First Samuel 4:17–18 we are told:

> So the messenger answered and said, "Israel has fled before the Philistines, and there has been a great slaughter among the people. Also your two sons, Hophni and Phinehas, are dead; and the ark of God has been captured." Then it happened, when he made mention of the ark of God, that Eli fell off the seat backward by the side of the gate; and his neck was broken and he died, for the man was old and heavy. And he had judged Israel forty years.

All the days of Eli, and all of the days of his sons, the Philistines took whatever they wanted from the covenant Israelites. There was no victory. There was hardly any blessing. Whatever they grew they could not keep because it was stolen. They endured forty years of loss. We ask ourselves, "Why?" As Christians in a nation founded for the purpose of religious freedom, why have we encountered decades of loss! Why was there such a dramatic transition between the priesthood of Eli and the priesthood of Samuel? The answer is that all the days of Samuel, God's hand was moved against the enemies of Israel. Why is God's hand not moved today? We have a new covenant based on better promises. When the early church faced a Herod, they moved God's hand. God's hand removed Herod. **Where is the church that moves God's hand?** Where is the priesthood like

Samuel's? Is it possible that our priesthood is more like Eli today than Samuel? The goal of Advanced Spiritual Flight Training is to make our character match the maneuvers we need to make. Our experience and character now become a part of the whole package. How we act on the ground twenty-four hours prior to flying dramatically affects our performance. Practicing aerial combat with a hangover could be an intestinally wrenching experience. The choices we make in how we conduct our lives can dramatically affect our performance.

First Samuel 2:12–14 reveals the reason Eli's priesthood could **not** move the hand of God:

> Now the sons of Eli were **corrupt**, they did not know the LORD. And the priests' custom with the people was that when any man offered a sacrifice, the priest's servant would come with a three–pronged flesh–hook in his hand while the meat was boiling. Then he would thrust it into the pan, or kettle, or caldron, or pot; and the priest would take **for himself all** that the flesh–hook brought up. So they did in Shiloh to all the Israelites who came there.

The priesthood did not follow God's ordinance in the ministry of the sacrifices. Nowhere did God ever invent *"a three–pronged flesh–hook"* by which to snag everything imaginable to satisfy personal greed! The spirit of mammon destroys our authority and renders our voice mute in the Throne Room of Heaven! Jesus made it very clear that there are two entities competing for worship – God the Creator and the spirit of mammon! Jesus said *"You **cannot** serve"* both; you have to make a choice! Whenever the priesthood is corrupted by the spirit of mammon, it cannot move the hand of God, nor teach the church to do so! Eli's corruption cost the nation for forty long years! Why is the church powerless when facing hostile government? The spirit of mammon has cost the church for forty long years! (For complete discussion of this issue see *Purifying the Altar,* available at **wordatwork.org**)

First Samuel 2:16–17 pretty much reflects the conditions we have today:

> And if the man said to him, "They should really burn the fat first; then you may take as much as your heart desires," he would then answer him, "No, but you must give it to me now; and if not, I will take it by force." Therefore the sin of the young men was very great before the LORD, for men abhorred the offering of the LORD.

There was so much manipulation in those days that people, when going to church, dreaded the offering. How many times today, whether in a conference or special meetings at church, do we dread the offering because the spirit of manipulation rules? How bad is it? God hasn't changed! He feels the same way about it today as He did in Eli's days. Verses 22–25 explain precisely how God feels:

> Now Eli was very old; and he heard everything his sons did to all Israel, and how they lay with the women who assembled at the door of the tabernacle of meeting. So he said to them, "Why do you do such things? For I hear of your evil dealings from all the people. No, my sons! For it is not a good report that I hear. You make the LORD's people transgress. If one man sins against another, God will judge him. But if a man sins against the LORD, who will intercede for him?" Nevertheless they did not heed the voice of their father, because the LORD **desired to kill them.**

Sexual immorality and the spirit of mammon destroy the integrity necessary to move God's hand. Ministry was so bad under Eli and his sons that **God determined** to kill them! God still removes people in ministry today when they have been eaten up by the spirit of mammon and refuse to change. He is the same yesterday, today, and forever! The leading candidates for Ananias and Sapphira events are generally found in the pulpit not the pew!

Advanced Flight Training is not for the faint of heart. It is for those who are determined to ascend into the heavenlies and touch the heart of God and move His hand. There is nothing quite like being cleared for take–off, getting in position, and applying max power! From that point on you know where you are going and its up up up! Isn't it time to go up up up into God's realm, experience God's power and apply it to make a **difference** in the condition of the church?

Where are the believers
Who move God's hand
So His holy purpose
Prevails in the land

Experience & character
Must act in conjunction
For justice & judgment
To work right & function

Chapter 18

Replacement Air Group

As soon as Advanced Flight Training was over, I was off to the Replacement Air Group, stationed at Moffet Field in Mountain View, California. This transition was major. Learning to set max take–off power by temperature seemed as strange as flaring at fifty feet for a landing. This transition was into jet engines and a platform about the size of a 737. I realized this equipment was designed to ferret out, find, track, and then destroy enemy submarines that were fully capable of nuking any city in America. We had a great platform, tremendous technology, and I got "dream" orders for a single guy—a two–year tour at Barbers Point, Hawaii, chasing subs. One day the Executive Officer of the squadron walked into our class and said, "I want two volunteers, preferably bachelors, for hazardous duty. The carrot is, I promise you will double your flight time. So if you want to be an airline pilot this is your opportunity."

I looked at my Polish friend from Nashua, New Hampshire, smiled and said, "Well, we want the air time." And in a moment of youthful inexperience I committed a major error—I volunteered. Within forty–eight hours my "dream" assignment was flushed away and my new assignment was VQ1 Agana, Guam. At least I chose one of the most technical squadrons in the Navy. Not everybody gets to fly a spy plane! Only four planes existed like the one I flew, and our squadron had two. The other two were dedicated to Europe! Suddenly I was no longer chasing subs. I was now headed for MIG and SAM threat warning, and had to be airborne anytime there was any air activity over North Vietnam. Sometimes we flew 240 hours in a month, 150 hours over the FAA maximum. That short thirty–second decision, in the lifting of my hand to volunteer, would end up becoming one and a half tours and 161 combat missions. By the time you get to Replacement Air Group, you start making decisions that affect your future for years to come.

Replacement Air Group has a parallel in today's spiritual warfare. That parallel is like what took place in the tabernacle of David. When the early church was debating in Acts 15 the issue of the Gentiles who were being saved and how much of the Law was going to apply to them, they found the Scripture in Amos describing the power of David's tabernacle and they said in verses 16–17:

> "After this I will return And will rebuild the tabernacle of David which has fallen down. I will rebuild its ruins, And I will set it up, So that the rest of mankind may seek the LORD, Even all the Gentiles who are called by My name," says the LORD who does all these things.

The tabernacle of David was one of the places where the covenant of "Sure Mercy" was used on a daily basis. The concept of continual worship and praise captures the foundation of David's tabernacle but not the real meat of what transpired there. David released covenant declarations on the worship and praise platform. The real meat of David's tabernacle is in the psalms he wrote. If we implemented continual worship and praise, but neglected the covenantal declarations prevalent in David's psalms, we would surely forfeit the fruit

David received! The fruit of the tabernacle was total victory on the battlefield for David and his army. If you were an enemy, you were headed for destruction. There was not a single enemy that could stand against David or his army and the key to understanding the spiritual dynamics of those victories is in what David wrote to be declared by the worshippers. His warfare psalms declare covenantal mercy for him manifested as destruction of the enemy. Acts 15 refers to David's tabernacle holding the key to winning nations! It is the reestablishing of what took place there that empowers the church to harvest nations as promised in Psalm 2, *"Ask of Me, and I will give You the nations. . . ."* God promises to rebuild it in the Spirit. The original passage in Amos 9:11–12 says:

> "On that day I will raise up The tabernacle of David, which has fallen down, And repair its damages; I will raise up its ruins, And rebuild it as in the days of old; That they may possess the remnant of Edom, And all the Gentiles who are called by My name," Says the Lord who does this thing.

It is obvious in this passage that the restoration of the tabernacle of David is what releases the authority to harvest all the nations. Therefore it is incumbent on us not only to look at the covenant of "Sure Mercy," but **how** David used it at that tabernacle and what he did when he first established it!

First Chronicles 16 is the account of commissioning the singers after the ark is returned to Jerusalem in chapter 15. First Chronicles 16:1–3 says:

> So they brought the ark of God, and set it in the midst of the tabernacle that David had erected for it. Then they offered burnt offerings and peace offerings before God. And when David had finished offering the burnt offerings and the peace offerings, he

blessed the people in the name of the LORD. Then he distributed to everyone of Israel, both man and woman, to everyone a loaf of bread, a piece of meat, and a cake of raisins.

David has the ark in Jerusalem and now the question is, what is he going to do? In verses 4–7 we find out:

And he appointed some of the Levites to minister before the ark of the LORD, to commemorate, to thank, and to praise the LORD God of Israel. Asaph the chief, and next to him Zechariah, then Jeiel, Shemiramoth, Jehiel, Mattithiah, Eliab, Benaiah, and Obed-Edom: Jeiel with stringed instruments and harps, but Asaph made music with cymbals; Benaiah and Jahaziel the priests regularly blew the trumpets before the ark of the covenant of God. And on that day David first delivered this psalm into the hand of Asaph and his brethren, to thank the LORD.

David appoints Levites and leaders to play and worship before the ark. The very first psalm that David gave to Asaph, in order to sing and proclaim, gives us the tenor of what took place there. There is worship, there is thanksgiving, there is praise, but notice verses 14–22:

He is the LORD our God; His judgments are in all the earth. Remember His **covenant** always, The word which He commanded, for a thousand generations, The **covenant** which He **made [kaw-rath]** with Abraham, And His oath to Isaac, And confirmed it to Jacob for a statute, To Israel for an everlasting covenant, Saying, "To you I will give the land of Canaan As the allotment of your inheritance," When you were but few in number, Indeed very few, and strangers in it. When they went from one nation to another, And from one kingdom to another people, He permitted no man to do them wrong; Yes, He reproved kings for their sakes, Saying, "Do not touch My anointed ones, And do My prophets no harm."

In verses 14 and 16 we find the words **ber-eeth** and **kaw-rath**. Verse 15 says, *"Remember his covenant always, The word which He commanded, for a thousand generations, The covenant which He* [**kaw-rath**] *cut/made with Abraham. . . ."* David had the covenant proclaimed consistently before God's presence. He declared in verse 33 that *". . . He is coming to judge the earth."* He proclaimed His mercy as enduring forever. In verse 35 He proclaimed that mercy to Israel meant deliverance from the enemy. David proclaimed covenant mercy through the Psalms declaring the judgment of God on the enemy. Praise and worship is valuable, but how much more if we use it as Psalm 149 presents it and as David practiced it!

For two years the Lord kept saying to me, "You don't know David. You don't know David. You don't know David. You don't know David. You don't know David." This is after thirty–plus years of studying God's Word. But I was in Spiritual Replacement Air Group Training. God was trying to give me a new platform to fly, to ferret out and bring destruction to the plans of the enemy with some entirely different technology. Different technology in the Spirit is the opening of our understanding to see what has been hidden in front of our face all the time.

Imagine while David was at war, Asaph was back before the ark singing, declaring, and decreeing covenant victory. David's psalms were sung. Psalms 52:1–5 says:

Why do you boast in evil, O mighty man? The goodness of God endures continually. Your tongue devises destruction, Like a sharp razor, working deceitfully. You love evil more than good, And lying rather than speaking righteousness. You love all devouring words,

You deceitful tongue. God shall likewise destroy you forever; He shall take you away, and pluck you out of your dwelling place, And uproot you from the land of the living.

If we are going to war, wouldn't we like to have somebody declaring covenant like this in our behalf? Today the battle is not only out on the field with an enemy that is often unidentifiable, but it is also at home with groups manifesting ideological malignancies like the "mainstream media" whose abhorrence of the church is manifested weekly. Imagine our Christian leaders singing this before the Lord as we face political battles at home. Psalm 54:1–5 says:

Save me, O God, by Your name, And vindicate me by Your strength. Hear my prayer, O God; Give ear to the words of my mouth. For strangers have risen up against me, And oppressors have sought after my life; They have not set God before them. Behold, God is my helper; The Lord is with those who uphold my life. He will repay my enemies for their evil. Cut them off in Your truth [or faithfulness].

The David I didn't know was the one who consistently wrote psalms declaring covenantal mercy cutting off whoever was an enemy. Covenant mercy for David meant total destruction for the enemy. It is really how he thought. God only manifested mercy for him when his enemy was under his feet. David was a warrior and he understood God's covenant of mercy. Mercy to him meant destruction to the enemy. Imagine Psalm 58:6–11 being continually proclaimed as we face hostile media or perverse politicians:

Break their teeth in their mouth, O God! Break out the fangs of the young lions, O Lord! Let them flow away as waters which run continually, When he bends his bow, Let his arrows be as if cut in pieces. Let them be like a snail which melts away as it goes, Like a stillborn child of a woman, that they may not see the sun. Before your pots can feel the burning thorns, He shall take them away as with a whirlwind, As in His living and burning wrath. The righteous shall rejoice when he sees the vengeance; He shall wash his feet in the blood of the wicked, So that men will say, "Surely there is a reward for the righteous; Surely He is God who judges in the earth."

David understood something. When there is no judgment, there is no justice! God has ordained His people to be agents of His government. One major governmental function is bringing righteous judgment! In Isaiah 9 we are told in verses 6–7:

For unto us a Child is born, Unto us a Son is given; And the government will be upon His shoulder. And His name will be called Wonderful, Counselor, Mighty God, Everlasting Father, Prince of Peace. Of the increase of His government and peace There will be no end, Upon the throne of David and over His kingdom, To order it and establish it with **judgment and justice** from that time forward, even forever. The zeal of the LORD of hosts will perform this.

Where is *"judgment and justice"* today? It is a function of God's government. Peter had no problem announcing the death of Ananias and Sapphira. There is a time for God's government and only God's government can bring justice to unreachable individuals who have been appointed for life–long terms. The church needs to release God's government on the ACLU who, through their local attorneys, consistently attempt to remove and silence anything Christian in the public arena. If the ACLU were suing your city to remove the cross from your emblem, as they did in Los Angeles, here is a possible way to pray:

Father, I invoke the covenant of "Sure Mercy" over Los Angeles [your region]. Have mercy on our land and cut off, dry up, reduce to zero, every source of financing for every ACLU attorney in our area. Break them in bankruptcy that they may be delivered from their idols to serve You. Restore the voice of the church as You dry up the voice of the wicked. Arise, O God, and let the fear of the Lord return to the land. In Your mercy *kaw-rath*, covenant the ACLU and bless, multiply, and empower Your church!" (Additional potential recommendation: As led pray Psalm 58:6–11 over CNN, CBS, NBC, ABC.)

There is nothing quite like Replacement Air Group Training. When we graduate we are qualified to fly the best our country has to offer! Are we qualified? Are we using the best that God has? Let the rebellious beware! The government of God is **rising!**

Did you know you are ordained
A "God-assigned" agent of change
"Kaw-rath"—cut off—move forth—destroy
All that the enemy would employ

Saint, rise up—extend your hand
For the saving of this land
Creation groans and needs to see
The church arise in victory

Chapter 19

Nuclear Weapons Delivery School

My next duty station was for five months at NAS, North Island. There is no place quite like Naval Air Station, North Island, Coronado, California. As a Midwestern boy growing up in the snow, I dreamed of balmy weather. In December and January, for the formerly snow–bound, to have seventy-five degree weather and be on a golf course is to feel like you died and went to heaven. That soon faded, however, in the face of the training that took place. Nuclear Weapons Delivery School spotlights the issue of learning your ordinance and how to deliver it. We studied the early nukes and the ones we were producing then, specifically the ones that could be fitted on our airplane to drop! I have to admit, of all the certificates of training I received, the diploma I am proudest of is my certificate from Nuclear Weapons Delivery School with my name appearing right in the middle of the mushroom cloud. Do we know our spiritual ordinance? Are we qualified to deliver it? Are we **willing** to deliver it? Can we practice dropping spiritual covenantal nukes in prayer? Any volunteers?

In Matthew 24:6–7 Jesus said we would have wars because *"nation would rise against nation and kingdom against kingdom."* How can the church be swayed by the anti–war sentiment of the cowardly peace–at–any–cost, including the surrender/negotiate with radical Islam crowd? When I look at the church today, I have to conclude, many are totally unaware of the possibility of even having ordinance, let alone knowing how to deliver it. Perhaps it is because we have had fifty years of ministry concentrating on Jesus in the gospels. The majority of believers in the church today do not **know** the resurrected, ascended, seated–at–the–right–hand KING of kings and LORD of lords. Jesus the Judge is ready to reveal Himself! Revelation 19:11 highlights the Jesus who dispenses spiritual nukes today:

> Then I saw heaven opened, and behold, a white horse. And He who sat on him was called Faithful and True, and in righteousness He judges and makes war.

Will we volunteer for the war Jesus is making? How deceived are sections of the church and their leaders who oppose all war in the name of the Lord! There are significant numbers of church leaders who don't know Jesus at all! If we don't know Jesus the Judge who makes war, we don't know God! Revelation 19:12–14 presents a good introduction:

> "His eyes were like a flame of fire, and on His head were many crowns. He had a name written that no one knew except Himself. He was clothed with a robe dipped in blood, and His name is called The Word of God. And the armies in heaven, clothed in fine linen, white and clean, followed Him on white horses."

Meet Jesus whose *"robe is dipped in blood"* while His army is clad in *"fine linen, white and clean."* This Jesus has been dispensing judgment up close and personal. Perhaps He has been "executing the judgment written" as proclaimed by the saints. A church that cannot move

God's hand is a church that has lost its salt. The Jesus we represent in the last days eliminates those who consistently oppose the harvest. Verses 15–17 describe the Jesus we represent:

> Now out of His mouth goes a sharp sword, that with it He should strike the nations. And He Himself will rule them with a rod of iron. He Himself treads the winepress of the fierceness and wrath of Almighty God. And He has on His robe and on His thigh a name written: KING OF KINGS AND LORD OF LORDS. Then I saw an angel standing in the sun; and he cried with a loud voice, saying to all the birds that fly in the midst of heaven, "'Come and gather together for the supper of the great God."

The entire book of Revelation was written so we could understand the ministry that Jesus entered once He had been resurrected, ascended and seated at the right hand of God. It is dramatically different from His ministry in the gospels. The seven churches in Revelation 2–3 would agree that the Jesus who ascended was far different from Jesus in the gospels. If we don't know both streams of Jesus' anointing, we are so lopsided as to be nearly worthless in the saving and redeeming of a nation!

In Mark 4:36–41 we find the comforting Jesus, who stills the storm. We are told:

> Now when they had left the multitude, they took Him along in the boat as He was. And other little boats were also with Him. And a great windstorm arose, and the waves beat into the boat, so that it was already filling. But He was in the stern, asleep on a pillow. And they awoke Him and said to Him, "Teacher, do You not care that we are perishing?" Then He arose and rebuked the wind, and said to the sea, "Peace, be still!" And the wind ceased and there was a great calm. But He said to them, "Why are you

so fearful? How is it that you have no faith?" And they feared exceedingly, and said to one another, "Who can this be, that even the wind and the sea obey Him!"

Jesus took His governmental authority and stopped a storm. Then He rebuked the Twelve for being so fearful and questioned why they couldn't do it themselves. Verse 41 highlights this issue as they contemplate Who it is, *"that even the winds and sea obey Him."* So in the gospels we see Jesus as the "stiller" of the storm.

Jesus the Judge is quite unhappy with what is happening at Pergamos. He says in Revelation 2:14–16:

> But I have a few things against you, because you have there those who hold the doctrine of Balaam, who taught Balak to put a stumbling block before the children of Israel, to eat things sacrificed to idols, and to commit sexual immorality. Thus you also have those who hold the doctrine of the Nicolaitans, which thing I hate. Repent, or else I will come to you quickly and will fight against them with the sword of My mouth.

If Jesus comes to *"fight against them with the sword of His mouth,"* a large storm would be generated. He is **sending** a storm . . . a storm that could have tremendous consequences personally.

In the gospels, Jesus stills the storm. In Revelation, He says, "If you don't repent I am going to send one." In Matthew 10:6–8 we see Jesus sending the Twelve and anointing them to *"heal the sick, cleanse the lepers, raise the dead, cast out demons."* He has obviously lit their candlestick with a great anointing. In Revelation 2:5, speaking to the church at Ephesus, He says, *"Remember therefore from where you have fallen; repent and do the first works, or else I will come to you quickly and remove your lampstand from its place—unless you repent."* In the gospels Jesus anoints the Twelve and sends them out. In Revelation

2 to the church at Ephesus He says, *"If you don't repent, I will take your anointing and put out your candlestick."*

What happened between the gospels and Revelation that so dramatically added a new dimension to the ministry of Jesus? In John 16:33 Jesus said, *"These things I have spoken to you, that in Me you may have peace. In the world you will have tribulation; but be of good cheer, I have overcome the world."* Jesus in the gospels promised that He would impart peace and with that peace we could overcome the tribulation that is in the world. In Revelation 2:22, to the church at Thyatira, He says, *"Indeed I will cast her into a sickbed, and those who commit adultery with her into **great tribulation**, unless they repent of their deeds."* Jesus in the gospels gives peace to overcome tribulation, but in Revelation 2 He says, *"If you don't repent I will send it."*

John 10:10 says, *"The thief does not come except for to steal, and to kill, and to destroy. I have come that they may have life, and that they may have it more abundantly."* To the church at Sardis, in Revelation 3:3, Jesus said, *"Remember therefore how you have received and heard; hold fast and repent. Therefore if you will not watch, I will come upon you as a thief, and you will not know what hour I will come upon you."* Jesus warns about the thief, which is the enemy in the gospels, but in Revelation He says, "If you don't repent, church, you don't have to worry about the enemy as a thief because I will come and take from you."

In Matthew 11:28 we are told, *"Come to Me, all you who labor and are heavy laden, and I will give you rest."* To the church at Laodicea, in Revelation 3:16 Jesus had this to say, *"So then, because you are lukewarm, and neither cold nor hot, I will spew you out of My mouth."* In the gospels He welcomes everybody. In Revelation 3 to the church at Laodicea He says, "If you don't repent you are history—you are out of here."

Why does Jesus go nuclear in Revelation? Because in Revelation He is the Judge of all the earth and a church that is not equipped to demonstrate Jesus the Judge is not equipped to walk with Him in the end–times. When Jesus called Peter to go nuclear in Acts 5, he didn't flinch, he didn't hesitate. I'm sure he remembered his certificate from Nuclear Weapons Delivery School and got mentally ready to flip the switch. Ananias and Sapphira died. The principle upon which all military training stands is both simple and biblical. Saving the nation means destroying the enemy. David understood this and prayed accordingly. If we can learn to pray against the enemy as David did, God will do the rest. Jesus is Judge of all the earth and quite capable of removing any foe!

The church today is quite familiar with Jesus in the gospels, but Jesus in Revelation is a foreigner, a stranger, completely and totally unknown. The fruit that we see in the church is no fear of God, and consequently there is none in the nation! How can the nation know Jesus the Judge if the church does not? Are our nations in the condition they are in today because we haven't known Jesus the Judge? Where is the church that can walk with Jesus in Revelation? Where is the church that does not flinch when Jesus kills a third of mankind? Revelation 9:18–19 says:

> By these three plagues a third of mankind was killed—by the fire and the smoke and the brimstone which came out of their mouths. For their power is in their mouth and in their tails; for their tails are like serpents, having heads; and with them they do harm.

In John 14, Jesus promised those who believed in Him would do the works He did and greater. A greater work than stilling a storm is generating one. A greater work than raising the dead is what Peter did with Ananis and Sapphira. The early church did the *"greater works."* Why aren't we?

There is very little fear of the Lord in the church and none in our politicians. Is the condition of the nation our fault? Are we in the mess we are in because we refused Father's military training? Where is Jesus the Judge? Is He waiting for representatives?

Hebrews 10:12–13 answers the question of why we don't see more of Jesus the Judge. *"But this Man, after He had offered one sacrifice for sins forever, sat down at the right hand of God, from that time waiting till His enemies are made His footstool."* He is waiting on us to take a stand on His covenant. When Isaiah saw Jesus' ministry, he saw the gospel ministry *and* Jesus in Revelation—together as a two–edged sword. Isaiah 61:1–3 says:

> The Spirit of the Lord GOD is upon Me, Because the LORD has anointed Me to preach good tidings to the poor; He has sent Me to heal the brokenhearted, To proclaim liberty to the captives, And the opening of the prison to those who are bound; To proclaim the acceptable year of the LORD, **And the day of vengeance of our God**; To comfort all who mourn, To console those who mourn in Zion, To give them beauty for ashes, The oil of joy for mourning, The garment of praise for the spirit of heaviness; That they may be called trees of righteousness, The planting of the LORD, that He may be glorified.

Jesus bought and paid for the anointing which heals, and covenant vengeance which releases that anointing. Chapter 35 encourages us to invoke the covenant over a church or ministry where mercy to man demonstrates judgment on the enemy, manifested through healing and deliverance. Isaiah 35:1–4 says:

> The wilderness and the wasteland shall be glad for them, And the desert shall rejoice and blossom as the rose; It shall blossom abundantly and rejoice, Even with joy and singing. The glory of Lebanon shall be given to it, The excellence of Carmel and Sharon. They shall see the glory of the LORD, The excellency of our God,

Strengthen the weak hands, And make firm the feeble knees, Say to those who are fearful–hearted, "Be strong, do not fear! Behold, your God will come with vengeance, With the recompense of God; He will come and save you."

We are prompted to invoke the covenant of "Sure Mercy", expecting a divine demonstration of Jesus triumphing and making a public display of principalities and powers, by releasing a healing anointing, which is described in verses 5–8:

Then the eyes of the blind shall be opened, And the ears of the deaf shall be unstopped. Then the lame shall leap like a deer, And the tongue of the dumb sing, For waters shall burst forth in the wilderness, And streams in the desert, The parched ground shall become a pool, And the thirsty land springs of water; In the habitation of jackals, where each lay, There shall be grass with reeds and rushes. A highway shall be there, and a road, And it shall be called the Highway of Holiness, The unclean shall not pass over it, But it shall be for others, Whoever walks the road, although a fool, Shall not go astray.

Imagine such an outpouring of Holy Spirit authority that no sickness or disease can stand in its presence! Even the foolishness of youth is held in check by the magnitude of God's presence! Invoking the covenant of "Sure Mercy" has a judgment side which reveals God's love, mercy, and restoration for physical infirmity. It's time to call down the fire!

Our glorious Jesus resurrected
Right-hand seated and ascended

Is so much more than His grace side
In Him the judgment sword abide

He doesn't flinch or hesitate
With His strong arm to set things straight

Saint, triumph there at Jesus side
Help turn our nation's foes aside

Chapter 20

SERE

Survival Evasion Resistance Escape

I loved North Island but then I went on Survival Evasion Resistance and Escape Training. After five days of the worst hell ever devised by man, I changed my mind. I wasn't sure I was still in America. The three days of prison camp we endured makes you believe at the end of it you are a prisoner of war. In my entire life, I was never so glad to graduate from anything as I was Survival Evasion Resistance and Escape. Eating bugs is easy compared to the torture phase. But once you are through it, you know what to expect and you really are psychologically ready for war. You know what your enemy is capable of and there are no illusions about what is ahead. It's a simple matter of "kill them before they kill us." If there was ever any hesitation in the thought of delivering nukes, it was eradicated never to be seen or heard from again. The compound phase of SERE was designed from the experiences of those who escaped from North Vietnam POW camps. I began thinking like a warrior where the enemy was concerned. I would have volunteered to nuke 'em!

One of the problems with the church today is we don't think in biblical terms. God is a man of war! David was a man of war after

God's own heart. And when David went to war, he made sure the covenant was continually being proclaimed before the ark at home. Perhaps we should apply the sevenfold test of doctrine to see if God really consistently expects us to move His hand in judgment. Moving God's hand is a two–edged sword. One edge *stops* judgment while the other *starts* it. When the Lord sent armies to war, there was no confusion about rules of engagement. The God who is willing, at man's request, to stop the sun for about a day so more of the enemy can be killed is our yardstick to measure thinking straight. There is only one Greek word to describe those who attempt to portray Jesus as a pacifist—**id-ee-o-tace**! If we were to rank miracles of the Bible, stopping the rotation of the universe would rate fairly high! We need to renew our mind to **think** like God thinks about war! How would God, who stopped the universe to aid Joshua's killing of the enemy, respond to our prayers in war? The church is in a spiritual war with a variety of demonized groups from the ACLU to Muslim extremists. Invoking the covenant of "Sure Mercy" and asking God to cut off a person who would destroy us if he could, just because we are Americans, almost seems like an honor. Asking God for covenant vengeance is asking for justice! It is an honor!

The sevenfold test requires we find an example of man moving God's hand in Genesis somewhere in seed form. In Genesis 18 God comes to visit Abraham and what He says reveals His very intention for relationship with man. In verse 17 God said:

> And the LORD said, "Shall I hide from Abraham what I am doing, since Abraham shall surely become a great and mighty nation, and all the nations of the earth shall be blessed in him? For I have known him, in order that he may command his children and his household after him, that they keep the way of the LORD, to do righteousness and justice, that the LORD may bring to Abraham what He has spoken to him."

God invited Abraham to move His hand! It is obvious Abraham moved God's hand because Lot and family were still lingering in the face of imminent destruction in chapter 19. Lot was pleading to go to this little city and not have to go to the mountains, when the angel said, in verse 22, *"'Hurry, escape there. For I cannot do anything until you arrive there.' Therefore the name of the city was called Zoar."* Abraham's intercession held the hand of judgment until Lot had escaped to Zoar. We have a better covenant based on better promises in the New Testament. Surely we can stop the hand of judgment over a region where we need a harvest. Test number one is satisfied in Genesis.

Test two asks, "Does what we see in Genesis in seed form have a fuller expression in the Pentateuch (law—Genesis to Deuteronomy)?" In Numbers 16 Moses was dealing with Korah, Dathan and Abiram. Verses 29–33 state:

> "If these men die naturally like all men, or if they are visited by the common fate of all men, then the LORD has not sent me. But if the LORD creates a new thing, and the earth opens its mouth and swallows them up with all that belongs to them, and they go down alive into the pit, then you will understand that these men have rejected the LORD." Then it came to pass, as he finished speaking all these words, that the ground split apart under them, and the earth opened its mouth and swallowed them up, with their households, and all the men with Korah, with all their goods. So they and all those with them went down alive into the pit; the earth closed over them, and they perished from among the congregation.

This passage presents precisely what happened. For all who would question whether it was Moses who moved the hand of God, verse 41 offers this view, *"On the next day all the congregation of the children of Israel murmured against Moses and Aaron, saying, 'You have killed the people of the LORD.'"*

Insights concerning the nuclear option are beginning to emerge. Apparently when individuals or nations yield to demons to the point they make God's purpose impossible to achieve, then these individuals, groups, or nations qualify for God's nuclear option. The nuclear option is judgment. It is not an issue of personality. It is not an issue of personal offense. It is an issue of demonically–motivated people who advance satan's cause while thwarting God's purpose! Korah, Dathan and Abiram qualified. Such a case could be made for a number of U.S. Supreme Court Justices. Either God moved Moses or Moses moved God's hand. It was accomplished without hesitation, without debate, without guilt and without remorse. It was an issue of leadership. It had to be done. Test number two is satisfied.

Test number three decrees we must find it in the Psalms or in the Proverbs. We find it in Psalm 149 as well as Psalm 143:12 where David said, *"In Your mercy cut off my enemies, And destroy all those who afflict my soul; For I am Your servant."* Psalm 149:7–9 says, *"executing covenant vengeance on the nations, And punishments on the peoples; To bind their kings with chains, And their nobles with fetters of iron; executing on them the judgment written is an honor for all the saints."* Perhaps it is time to take this honor a bit more seriously.

For test four, did the prophets move the hand of God in judgment? Isaiah 37:14 is a classic. The Assyrian army and its leader brought to Jerusalem a letter of reproach, to be read in the hearing of all the people before finding its way to Hezekiah. Isaiah 37:14–17 chronicles the king's response:

And Hezekiah received the letter from the hand of the messengers, and read it; and Hezekiah went up to the house of the LORD, and spread it before the LORD. Then Hezekiah prayed to the LORD, saying: "O LORD of hosts, God of Israel, the One who dwells between the cherubim, You are God, You alone, of all the kingdoms of the earth. You have made heaven and earth. Incline Your ear, O LORD, and hear; open Your eyes, O LORD, and see; and hear all the words of Sennacherib, who has sent to reproach the living God."

In verse 21 we see God's view of King Hezekiah's prayer, *"Then Isaiah the son of Amoz sent to Hezekiah, saying, 'Thus says the LORD God of Israel, "Because you have **prayed to Me against** Sennacherib king of Assyria."'"* For fifty years we have been taught **not** to *"pray against"* people. Could God ever say to us, "because you prayed to Me **against** the ACLU"; "because you prayed to Me **against** People For The American Way"; "because you prayed to Me **against** the homosexual lesbian agenda." Praying for the bankruptcy of liberally–biased media which, in my opinion, persistently and politically pervert the slant of their stories, is a godly governmental call. One day we should hear from our Father, "because you prayed to Me **against** CNN, I am putting them out of business." When media organizations broadcast enemy propaganda and consistently demonstrate an Antichrist agenda, they should be prayed out of business. It is time to recognize the propaganda machines of the enemy and move God's hand to close them down. The arrogant Antichrist news media need to meet Jesus the Judge. Has God ever heard us pray with the heart of David or the heart of Hezekiah? Have we ever invoked the covenant of "Sure Mercy"? Is it possible for us to get a response from God because we ask Him to remove those who are standing in the way of His purposes? God's response to Hezekiah was pretty straightforward. Isaiah 37:21–22,33–35 says:

> Then Isaiah the son of Amoz sent to Hezekiah, saying, "Thus says the LORD God of Israel, 'Because you have prayed to Me against

Sennacherib king of Assyria, this is the word which the LORD has spoken concerning him: The virgin, the daughter of Zion, Has despised you, laughed you to scorn; The daughter of Jerusalem has shaken her head behind your back!'" Therefore thus says the LORD concerning the king of Assyria: "He shall not come into this city, Nor shoot an arrow there, Nor come before it with shield, Nor build a siege mound against it. By the way that he came, By the same shall he return; And he shall not come into this city." Says the LORD. "For I will defend this city, to save it For My own sake and for My servant David's sake."

Wouldn't it be nice to get an answer from God that said "because you prayed to Me against this, I have answered you for the sake of My servant David and his covenant of 'Sure Mercy'"? "Because you have prayed to Me against the treasonous, treacherous senators who try to decimate the military, and are more concerned about the rights of criminals and terrorists than their victims, I have heard and will remove them." We need to hear what Hezekiah heard. Perhaps even sweeter for Hezekiah was knowing that God not only answered, but He didn't hesitate in bringing judgment. Verse 36 says, *"Then the angel of the LORD went out and killed in the camp of the Assyrians one hundred and eighty-five thousand; and when people arose early in the morning, there were the corpses—all dead."* If Hezekiah could move God's hand and He is no respecter of persons—why can't we?

Let's continue with the sevenfold test to see if God expects us to move His hand in judgment. Test number five is, Did Jesus teach it? One of the things that is popular for people to ask is, "What would Jesus do?" When demonized individuals choose to destroy a city directly or allow the perversion that fills the land with iniquity (homosexual marriage), we have a spiritual governmental obligation to move God's hand and preserve the city for a harvest! In this situation, Jesus certainly would not turn the other cheek. This is a governmental issue because it presents a hindrance to the ordained harvest. Therefore, if we take our governmental responsibilities seriously, like Moses, or like Hezekiah, we have an obligation to invoke the covenant of "Sure Mercy." Let God have mercy on the nation and cut off those who are attempting to destroy it. We want a harvest out of this country. In Luke 18:1–7 Jesus said:

> Then He spoke a parable to them, that men always ought to pray and not lose heart, saying: "There was in a certain city a judge who did not fear God nor regard man. Now there was a widow in that city; and she came to him, saying, 'Avenge me of my adversary.' And he would not for a while; but afterward he said within himself, 'Though I do not fear God nor regard man, yet because this widow troubles me I will avenge her, lest by her continual coming she weary me.' Then the Lord said, "Hear what the unjust judge said. And shall God not avenge His own elect who cry out day and night to Him, though He bears long with them?"

In verses 3 and 5 in speaking to the unjust judge, Jesus uses for "avenge" **ek-dik-eh-o**, meaning to retaliate or punish. The point of the parable is obvious. Unjust judges prolong answering pleas for justice. Just judges like God do not. When Jesus speaks of His Father answering pleas for justice, He uses **ek-dik-a-sis**, the technical term for administrative justice. The picture presented is, when we call shall we not get an administrative decision from God Himself? Verse 8 is the kicker because in verse 8 Jesus directly challenges those of us who live in this generation when He says, *"I tell you that He will avenge them speedily. Nevertheless, when the Son of Man comes, will He really find faith on the earth?"* In Greek there is a definite article that appears before "faith" so it really says, *"When the Son of Man comes, will He really find **this kind** of faith on the earth?"* Jesus questioned whether

He would find faith that obtains an administrative decision releasing judgment that removes obstacles to the end–time harvest! *"Ask of Me and I will give you the nations. . . ."* Does this kind of faith exist in the church? Jesus challenged us. He wasn't sure. He wanted to know when He comes if He will find it. That is as much encouragement as I need to move in this direction. Jesus taught it!

Test six is, Can we find an example in Acts? In the book of Acts did anybody move the hand of God in judgment? Either Peter moved the hand of God or the hand of God moved Peter in the death of Ananias and Sapphira. Assuming that most of us will look at that as the hand of God moving Peter, we need to go to Acts 12. In the first four verses Herod the king killed James, the brother of John. He incarcerated Peter. The church began to pray. Demonized Herod was trying to stop the purpose and plan of God, not very different from what Korah, Dathan and Abiram did. This situation is no different than Hezekiah and Sennacherib. The church prayed, the angel came, and Peter got out of jail, after which Herod continued in his ways. The angel came again and the most painful death known to man fell upon Herod. Verse 23 records, *"Then immediately an angel of the Lord struck him, because he did not give glory to God. And he was eaten by worms and died."* Herod's death was not an accident. The text reveals divine intervention. To think that divine intervention is not connected to what the church prayed is to qualify for the title "Spiritual Space Cadet." The early church moved God's hand! Why can't we? The Antichrist decisions from the Supreme Court limiting the church's voice can stop if we move God's hand on the offending Justices. God is ready, all the church need do is **ASK**!

"The Word is near us, even in our mouth. . . ." Jesus the Judge is as close as the words we speak. Suppose we have Supreme Court Justices who champion every perverse thing imaginable and continue filling our land with iniquity through abortion—how should we pray? Here is a suggestion:

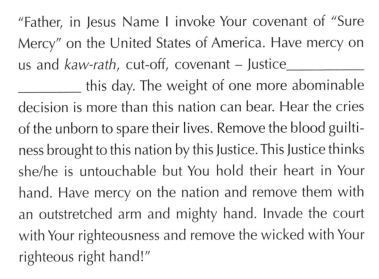

"Father, in Jesus Name I invoke Your covenant of "Sure Mercy" on the United States of America. Have mercy on us and *kaw-rath*, cut-off, covenant – Justice_____ _____ this day. The weight of one more abominable decision is more than this nation can bear. Hear the cries of the unborn to spare their lives. Remove the blood guiltiness brought to this nation by this Justice. This Justice thinks she/he is untouchable but You hold their heart in Your hand. Have mercy on the nation and remove them with an outstretched arm and mighty hand. Invade the court with Your righteousness and remove the wicked with Your righteous right hand!"

Number seven is, Can we find it in the Epistles? Second Timothy 4:14–15 state, *"Alexander the coppersmith did me much harm. May the Lord repay him according to his works. You also must beware of him, for he has greatly resisted our words."* What did Paul ask for? He asked for God to *"repay him according to his works."* Can there be any doubt what the apostle had in mind? Paul had a previous encounter. First Timothy 1:18–20 says:

> This charge I commit to you, son Timothy, according to the prophecies previously made concerning you, that by them you may wage the good warfare, having faith and a good conscience, which some having rejected, concerning the faith have suffered shipwreck, of whom are Hymenaeus and Alexander, whom **I delivered to Satan** that they may learn not to blaspheme.

Paul delivered Alexander to satan for the destruction of his flesh. That was in round one. In round two, Second Timothy records Paul praying to *"repay him according to his works."* Is there any doubt that the apostle Paul believed he could move the hand of God against those who were hindering God's purpose? This was ***not*** a personal offense issue. It was a matter of, "You are stopping God's purpose for this region, for this city, for this nation, therefore I have no choice but to move God's hand against you." God expects us to move His hand. It is an issue of spiritual government. Paul moved God's hand against offenders within the church and against those outside the church. The government of God was an integral part of the apostolic culture. As this culture is restored to the church, at least we know a little of what to expect.

Perhaps the final thing we need to look at is Ephesians 6, to help us with spiritual perspective concerning this issue. Ephesians 6:10–12 says:

> Finally, my brethren, be strong in the LORD and in the power of His might. Put on the whole armor of God, that you may be able to stand against the wiles of the devil. For we do not wrestle against flesh and blood, but against principalities, against powers, against the rulers of the darkness of this age, against spiritual hosts of wickedness in the heavenly places.

The fact that *"we do not wrestle against flesh and blood but against principalities and powers, against the rulers of the darkness"* tells us that when we invoke the covenant of "Sure Mercy" or claim mercy for the nation and ask God to cut off the demonized offending parties, our intent is that they be cut off from the demonic influences that are using them. We hope they choose deliverance and salvation. Their demonized choices form the foundation for invoking the covenant of "Sure Mercy." We are obligated to demand an end to the defiling destroying fruit of their choices. We refuse to lose a nation due to the actions of a few. Once the covenant is invoked, their choices are not our issue. If they refuse to separate, then there is no choice but for God to remove them, but that is not our issue—it is His. The only safe way to enter this dimension is to consistently yield to the Holy Spirit. The same Holy Spirit who led the early church in their warfare leads us. He is the same yesterday, today and forever. He has not changed. He will do for us, when we face a Herod, what He did for them. He will do for us, when we face an Elymas, what he did for Paul. He will do for us when we face superior authority, what He did for Hezekiah.

No greater example exists today than the radical Islamic Imams and their disciples who lead nations. They have openly stated that their purpose is to completely and totally annihilate Israel. In Romans 11, God promised to give us the Jews as the last people–group to be grafted into the vine. Now we have nations of people whose stated purpose is to destroy the harvest that God has promised biblically. We have no choice but to initiate the spiritual nuclear option. Moses knew he could not complete his assignment if Korah, Dathan and Abiram destroyed all progress; God's hand was moved and the perpetrators descended alive into the pit. Hezekiah knew he could not continue in the face of Assyria's threats. When the Son of Man returns will He find this kind of faith in the earth? It is time to take a stand to invoke the covenant of "Sure Mercy." Ask God to have mercy on Israel by cutting off all those who would destroy that harvest. Invoking the covenant of "Sure Mercy" is an issue of faith. In light of the biblical promises and the demonized people who are threatening to destroy both the United States and Israel, what other option do we have?

When we graduate from Survival Evasion Resistance and Escape—we know, that we know, that we know that we are in a war and in that war we either dispose of the enemy or we lose our freedom, our life and possibly our land. It is *time* to get serious about war! It is time to use the weapons we have been given, without hesitation and without reservation!

It is time for the church to walk with Jesus the Judge and let God BE GOD.

Are you ready to act
Without hesitation
Are you serious in war
With no reservation

The same Holy Spirit
That led long ago
He'll guide every step
And God's strategy show

Chapter 21

Making the Transition

For a semi–pacifistic church to transition from "turn the other cheek" mentality into the governmental exercise of authority necessary to be Davidic is no small undertaking. How do we grow from where we are to where we need to be? The answer has already been provided by God's own Spirit. The Holy Spirit knows the way and offers a path to the Promised Land. Ephesians 5:18 says, *"And do not be drunk with wine, in which is dissipation; but be filled with the Spirit, speaking. . . ."* The biblical definition of being *"filled with the Spirit"* has a very specific purpose that is outlined in Ephesians 1. In Ephesians 1:13–14 we are told:

> In Him you also trusted, after you heard the word of truth, the
> gospel of your salvation; in whom also, having believed, you were
> sealed with the Holy Spirit of promise, who is the guarantee of
> our inheritance until the redemption of the purchased possession,
> to the praise of His glory.

Our inheritance is God Himself and comes via the Holy Spirit who takes up residence in our lives. Being *"filled with the Spirit"* has its own definition in Scripture. The best dictionary for Bible terms is the Bible. When Ephesians 5 says *"be filled with the Spirit,"* all we have to do is search for the first and subsequent places they were filled with the Spirit and see precisely what Scripture is recommending. Acts 2:1–4 says:

> Now when the Day of Pentecost had fully come, they were all with one accord in one place. And suddenly there came a sound from heaven, as of a rushing mighty wind, and it filled the whole house where they were sitting. Then there appeared to them divided tongues, as of fire, and one sat upon each of them. And they were all filled with the Holy Spirit and began to speak with other tongues, as the Spirit gave them utterance.

When they were filled with the Holy Spirit they began to speak in other tongues. They were given a prayer language and that prayer language had a very definite purpose. Some confusion has arisen in the evangelical world over the issue of tongues, when First Corinthians 12 is brought into view. In First Corinthians 12 the nine gifts of the Spirit are outlined and one of those gifts is tongues, requiring interpretation when manifested in a public meeting. Nowhere in this passage does *"be filled"* appear. It just speaks of the manifestation of the gifts of the Holy Spirit. These gifts of the Spirit that are manifested in a public setting are far different from the prayer language that was given in Acts 2. Throughout the book of Acts whenever people were filled with the Spirit they received a prayer language or it is implied in the context. There is a reason for a prayer language. And the prayer language is far different from speaking forth in tongues in a public setting where an interpretation is required.

Because of cessationist teaching against the gifts of the Spirit, there are a number of people who have asked to be filled with the Spirit but have not entered into their prayer language. The prayer language is essential and it is available to everyone who is born again. Availability to all is clearly seen in Acts 2:38–39. Verses 32–35 state:

> This Jesus God has raised up, of which we are all witnesses. There-fore being exalted to the right hand of God, and having received from the Father the promise of the Holy Spirit, He poured out this which you now see and hear. For David did not ascend into the heavens, but he says himself: "The LORD said to my Lord, 'Sit at My right hand, Till I make Your enemies Your footstool.'"

It is interesting that Peter's explanation of what God did when He filled them with the Spirit was the quoting of Psalm 110:1, *"The LORD said to my Lord, 'Sit at My right hand, Till I make Your enemies Your footstool.'"*

Being filled with the Spirit and using the prayer language initiates this heart–cry for the government of God to make our *"enemies our footstool."* Peter went on to say in verses 38–39, *"Repent, and let every one of you be baptized in the name of Jesus Christ for the remission of sins; and you shall receive the gift of the Holy Spirit. For the promise is to you and to your children, and to all who are afar off, as many as the Lord our God will call."* Peter made it plain that the same way they received the Holy Spirit was available to everyone who called upon the name of the Lord. That includes tongues because there is a specific reason for those tongues. That reason aids what we have already found in Ephesians. The empowering of the Spirit brings us a prayer language which may be one of the most practical things God has ever given! First Corinthians 14:1–2 says:

> Pursue love, and desire spiritual gifts, but especially that you may prophesy. For he who speaks in a tongue does not speak to men but to God, for no one understands him; however, in the spirit he speaks **mysteries**.

Isn't it interesting that the **mystery** that the church is going to manifest and declare to principalities and powers in Ephesians is now something that we are given the supernatural ability to request beyond our ability to understand or reject? We know this is the prayer language because verse 14 says, *"For if I pray in a tongue, my spirit prays, but my understanding is unfruitful."* The genius of a prayer language is that when we use it we allow God to ask for the full measure of our contribution to the mystery, even if our mind does not believe we are qualified or capable. Yet we can still ask for it in the Spirit! Asking for God's government to reign extends the Kingdom.

Paul goes on to say in verse 15 what we also find in Ephesians 5. *"What is the result then? I will pray with the spirit, and I will also pray with the understanding. I will sing with the spirit, and I will also sing with the understanding."* Paul said, "I will . . . I will . . . I will . . . I will—I choose to do this because it is a path to bringing mysteries out of the realm of the Spirit and into manifestation in the natural. It is a way to gain revelation. It is God–ordained. It is God–given, and I choose to do it."

First Corinthians 14:3–4 says, *"But he who prophesies speaks edification and exhortation and comfort to men. He who speaks in a tongue edifies himself, but he who prophesies edifies the church."* The Greek word for "edifies" is **oy-kod-om-eh-o.** It comes from **oy-kod-om-os,** meaning "to restore or repair by building; to set or repair the foundation; to promote growth." When we pray in tongues, we are restoring or repairing our spiritual house. We are setting or repairing the foundation. We are promoting growth. Tongues is a language of the Spirit, one we cannot allow to fall into disuse. Verse 16 says, *"Otherwise, if you bless with the spirit, how will he who occupies the place of the uninformed* [**id-ee-o-tace**] *say 'Amen' at your giving of thanks, since he does not understand what you say?"* When we pray in the Spirit we *"bless."* The Greek word is **yoo-log-eh-o.**

Yoo is an intensive. **Log-eh-o** comes from **log-os**. So together this word means intensely asking or declaring that part of the Word which the Spirit has ordained us to walk in. When we are praying in tongues, we are asking or declaring that part of the **log-os** which God wants to impart to us, ultimately placing His enemies under our feet. This is not the only place we find this, which reinforces why Paul, in Ephesians, tells us to *"be filled with the Spirit."* Seasons of transition offer the greatest opportunity for spiritual advancement through tongues. Praying in tongues can expedite such a transition, supernaturally positioning us for God's very best! Birth God's government—***PRAY IN THE SPIRIT!***

Jude 17–21 states:

> But you, beloved, remember the words which were spoken before by the apostles of our Lord Jesus Christ: how they told you that there would be mockers in the last times who would walk according to their own ungodly lusts. These are sensual persons, who cause divisions, not having the Spirit. But you, beloved, building yourselves up on your most holy faith, praying in the Holy Spirit, keep yourselves in the love of God, looking for the mercy of our Lord Jesus Christ unto eternal life.

Again we are told that we build ourselves up on our most holy faith when we are praying in the Spirit. First Corinthians 12 defines praying in the Spirit as praying in tongues.

Victory over the world, victory over division, and victory over strife is available through tongues. How many times are we tempted to be really offended within the Body of Christ, or with our own family, or within our workplace, but we are told that through tongues, in verse 21, we can *"keep ourselves in the love of God, looking for the mercy of our Lord Jesus unto eternal life."* Since offense and strife often come with a supernatural demonic element, overcoming them requires a supernatural Holy Spirit element. Staying in unity and staying in harmony can be victoriously won through tongues. Is it any wonder then, that Zephaniah 3:9 says, *"For then I will restore to the peoples a pure language, That they all may call on the name of the LORD, To serve Him with one accord."* That *"pure language"* is tongues because it expresses God's will. When we use it, what we ask is untainted by human emotion or fleshly desire. We enable or empower ourselves to stay in unity, stay in harmony, to forgive strife and offense and overcome it as *"the love of God is shed abroad in our heart by the Holy Spirit."* Praying in tongues can be just like dropping a bucket in a deep well. We can draw living water from very deep wells!

Another area of application that is absolutely essential, according to Isaiah 28:9–12 is that tongues facilitates transitions, when God is trying to move us from one dimension to another and we should use it for that purpose. Isaiah 28:9–12 says:

Whom will he teach knowledge? And whom will he make to understand the message? Those just weaned from milk? Those just drawn from the breast? For precept must be upon precept, precept upon precept, Line upon line, line upon line, Here a little, there a little. For with stammering lips and another tongue He will speak to this people, To whom He said, "This is the rest with which You may cause the weary to rest," And, "This is the refreshing"; Yet they would not hear.

We find this is the rest, this is the refreshing but *"they would not hear."* So tongues facilitates transitions by building us up in the Spirit, by bringing into the natural realm that which God is longing to reveal from the Spirit, and revealing His purposes and plans so we can say "yes." We can begin to move toward them and we can call into existence the full measure of God's ability to walk out the divine plan when it is revealed. Perhaps the most practical thing God ever gave the church was a prayer language to facilitate our union with Him and our harmony with each other. Are we using what God has given for the purpose to which it was ordained?

Ephesians 5 makes it a command, *"Be filled with the Spirit."* Translation: **use your prayer language.** It will take you from one season to another. It will help build and fortify your house. It will solidify the foundation. It will bring an understanding of God's purpose releasing power to walk it out.

In Acts 2:32–35 when Peter is listing the scriptural justifications for what God had just done concerning tongues, he says:

> This Jesus God has raised up, of which we are all witnesses. There-fore being exalted to the right hand of God, and having received from the Father the promise of the Holy Spirit, He poured out this which you now see and hear. For David did not ascend into the heavens, but he says himself: "The LORD said to my Lord, 'Sit at My right hand, Till I make Your enemies Your footstool.'"

It is obvious Peter received a revelation about tongues facilitating a birth of divine authority which releases manifestations of enemies being made a footstool. Tongues calls forth spiritual government which triumphs in the face of demonically–inspired natural govern-ment, whenever the two come into conflict. These two kingdoms are in conflict!

Perhaps to gain further understanding of what Peter had in mind, we should go back and look at Psalm 110 and read this quote in its original context. Psalm 110:1–2 says:

> The LORD said to my Lord, "Sit at My right hand, Till I make Your enemies Your footstool." The LORD shall send the rod of Your strength out of Zion. Rule in the midst of Your enemies!

Verse 2 makes it very clear that the context is definitely governmental. He says, *"The LORD shall send the rod of Your strength out of Zion. Rule in the midst of Your enemies!"* The *"rod of strength"* would be the scepter of a king and that scepter was extended at the discretion of a king whenever someone came forward for an audience. If a person was bold enough to approach without being called and the scepter was not extended, they were usually executed. If the scepter was extended, they were heard. A divine scepter has been extended. The kingly anointing for spiritual government is here. Spiritual government trumps that which we have in the natural. Verse 3 makes it clear that this authority is given to believers when it says, *"Your people shall be volunteers in the day of Your power; In the beauties of holiness, from the womb of the morning, You have the dew of Your youth."* We would ask how committed is God to bringing this to pass? Verse 4 says, *"The LORD has sworn and will not relent, 'You are a priest forever According to the order of Melchizedek.'"* Apparently what Jesus paid for and implemented would *". . . forever . . ."* be available to the church. As our High Priest and King, the scepter is always extended to the believer. Verses 5–6 state:

> The Lord is at Your right hand; He shall execute kings in the day of His wrath. He shall judge among the nations, He shall fill the places with dead bodies, He shall execute the heads of many countries. He shall drink of the brook by the wayside; Therefore He shall lift up the head.

As the resurrected, ascended, seated–at–the–right hand King of kings and Lord of lords, Jesus is Judge of all creation. In this passage, Jesus established government through conflict with kings, judges, and rulers of nations who knowingly, arbitrarily and rebelliously hinder His church. When leaders defile their nations, judgments are inevitable. The context of what was given to us in the gift of the Holy Spirit is a manifestation of government which makes our enemies our footstool and must be **prayed** into existence.

The number "7" is the number of completion, fulfillment, or perfection. Seven times this verse—about our enemies becoming our footstool—is either directly quoted or alluded to in the New Testament. The first appearance is in Matthew 22:34–40 which states:

> But when the Pharisees heard that He had silenced the Sadducces, they gathered together. Then one of them, a lawyer, asked Him a question, testing Him, and saying, "Teacher, which is the great commandment in the law?" Jesus said to him, "You shall love the LORD your God with all your heart, with all your soul, and with all your mind. This is the first and great commandment And the second is like it: You shall love your neighbor as yourself. On these two commandments hang all the Law and the Prophets."

Jesus finds Himself in verbal combat with the leaders of the religious sects of His day because they are polluting the temple and His job is to cleanse it. Once He had silenced the Sadducees, the Pharisees came after Him. The question is, how did He silence these groups? We get a picture of the process in verses 41–46. It says:

> While the Pharisees were gathered together, Jesus asked them, saying, "What do you think about the Christ? Whose Son is He?" They said to Him, "The Son of David." He said to them, "How then does David in the Spirit call Him "Lord," saying: 'The LORD said to my Lord, "Sit at My right hand, Till I make Your enemies Your footstool." If David then calls Him "Lord," how is He his Son?" And no one was able to answer Him a word, nor from that day on did anyone dare question Him anymore.

Jesus used Psalm 110:1 to silence the Pharisees. Interestingly enough when the Word and the Spirit are joined together, demonic delusion is silenced and can no longer speak! It is almost as if the fear of God fell upon them and they could no longer speak in His presence. Will that be a welcomed manifestation in the days ahead? I suspect it will and one we need to believe into manifestation.

The second account of Jesus using Psalm 110 is a parallel passage in Mark 12:35–40. Interestingly enough the same Scripture Jesus uses to silence the Pharisees has an entirely different impact on the common people. Isn't it interesting that the same Spirit and Word delivered together could completely and totally offend a religious spirit and have exactly the opposite affect on the common people who were not so infected?

Luke 20:39–44 describes the same event. It says:

Then some of the scribes answered and said, "Teacher, You have spoken well." But after that they dared not question Him any-more. And He said to them, "How can they say that the Christ is David's Son? Now David himself said in the Book of Psalms, 'The Lord said to my Lord, "Sit at My right hand, Till I make Your enemies Your footstool." David therefore calls Him 'Lord'; how is He then his Son?

Jesus silences the religious governmental authorities, but then He goes a step further. He uses it for a platform to draw a sign or warning for the people. Verses 45–47 state:

Then in the hearing of all the people, He said to His disciples, "Beware of the scribes, who desire to walk in long robes, love greetings in the marketplaces, the best seats in the synagogues, and the best places at feasts, who devour widows' houses, and for a pretense make long prayers. These will receive greater condemnation [or judgment]."

Now Jesus is connecting Psalm 110:1 with future manifestations of judgment. Obviously each account brings another aspect into view of the victorious church and the emerging spiritual governmental authority that Jesus is depositing among those who believe.

The fourth appearance is one we have already looked at in Acts 2:35 where the Holy Spirit is promised as the agent executing God's will governmentally through the church!

The fifth appearance is in Romans 16:17–20. It says:

> Now I urge you, brethren, note those who cause divisions and offenses, contrary to the doctrine which you learned, and avoid them. For those who are such do not serve our Lord Jesus Christ, but their own belly, and by smooth words and flattering speech deceive the hearts of the simple. For your obedience has become known to all. Therefore I am glad on your behalf; but I want you to be wise in what is good, and simple concerning evil. And the **God of peace will crush Satan under your feet** shortly. The grace of our Lord Jesus Christ be with you. Amen.

Isn't it interesting that Jesus says, *"The God of peace will crush Satan under your feet shortly."* Peace with each other, forgiveness, harmony, unity and maintaining one accord are absolutely essential for the manifestation of Spirit–led government in our midst. Unless we are willing to love each other and live in harmony within the church, how can we expect manifestations of divine government? Disagreement, disharmony and strife invalidate or completely spoil the promise of governmental anointing. There is a reason why we must love each other and choose to overlook inconsequential disagreements of doctrine. I choose to believe the government of God is more important than minor doctrinal disagreements.

The sixth appearance of "our enemies becoming our footstool" is in Hebrews 1:13–14. This passage says, *"But to which of the angels has He ever said: 'Sit at My right hand, Till I make Your enemies Your footstool'? Are they not all ministering spirits sent forth to minister for those who will inherit salvation?"* Another piece of the picture now begins to fit together. Not only do we access divine government through praying in our prayer language, but we also birth an authority angels are assigned to enforce when serving Father's purposes. This view gives us a spiritual background for what happened in Acts 12 when the church prayed and judgment eventually fell on Herod at the hands of a dispatched angel.

The seventh and final appearance of Psalm 110:1 is in Hebrews 10:12–13, *"But this Man, after He had offered one sacrifice for sins forever, sat down at the right hand of God, from that time waiting till His enemies are made His footstool."* Jesus is seated at the right hand of God and *"waiting"* for manifestations of divine government to come through the church. We can ultimately conclude that such manifestations will fulfill the harvest of the Gentiles and make the Jew jealous. The end–time church obviously walks in a spectacular anointing and in the process teaches principalities and powers the wisdom of God! Are we using what God has given us, or are we allowing this prayer language to be stolen through lack of use? A time of great spiritual authority is about to burst forth and we need to encourage each other to possess it through prayer!

Tongues is an essential weapon of war—**use it or lose it!**

That which is beyond my mind
Or finite comprehension
That which transcends human thoughts
Or my limited expression

Comes because I yield my tongue
To One I trust and know
God guides my prayers in languages
To move in His own flow

And I'll flow in authority
As God's volunteer
Disarming foes thru heavenly prayer
As the King draws near

PURIFYING THE ALTAR

Some of the most amazing covenantal promises in Scripture concern money and how we handle it. If we pass the mammon test, we can participate in spiritual government executing a judgment entitled the "Anointing to Spoil." Without cleansing the temple, the authority for spiritual government is lost.

The only place in Scripture where God invites us to **put Him to the test** is in the context of our choices with money. Malachi 3:10 states, *"Bring all the tithes into the storehouse. . . ."* By emphasizing the personal choice of giving as the determinant covenant factor we have missed half of what the Bible teaches on this subject, and consequently closed the windows of heaven. Instead of purifying the altar, we have hindered the church.

Jesus stated in Matthew 23, *"'Fools and blind! For which is greater, the gift or the altar that sanctifies the gift?'"* Jesus made the condition of the altar the determinant covenant factor. When an altar is cleansed so that it "sanctifies" what is given, the windows of heaven open. The covenant is then consummated.

Purifying the Altar is a study of the biblical principles which contribute to closing or opening the windows of heaven through purifying both the personal and corporate altars!

The following questions are answered.

1. What transpires in the realm of the spirit when we do business with God at an impure altar?
2. In every Bible–believing congregation, the majority of people agree, "We tithe and are doing the best we know to do, but we do not see the windows of heaven opened to the full extent God promised." Why?
3. The spiritual law of the altar states, the condition of the altar where we attend, participate and put our money is reproduced in our life, whether we are aware of it or not.

MARKED MEN

God has promised end–time protections for His people as we navigate perilous times to accomplish a great end–time harvest. The prophetic tragedy of the last leadership generation is that they equipped the church to recognize the mark of the counterfeit christ. The Bible promises nine real marks from the true Christ, each available for a specific end–time purpose. Almost every believer knows the counterfeit 666, but how many of us can name one of God's nine real marks enabling us to finish our call. Some of the questions answered are:

1. If in the end people must acquiesce to buy or sell, what must we do to achieve God's promised protection now?
2. If the cup has to be full before we get a new heavens and earth, doesn't this make the pre–trib, mid– and post– arguments inconsequential?
3. Should we expect the Christians who finish the age to pay less of a price than those who began it?
4. Are we preparing our children for the wrong rapture? How should we be training them for the future?
5. Will Jesus come *to* the church before He comes *for* it, and if so, for what purpose?
6. How does the principle of **fullness** impact the church? Does fullness of iniquity demand fullness of Christ?

CONVERTS OR DISCIPLES?

Converts or Disciples? is a prophetic word to the church, hopefully causing a reassessment of our ultimate purpose. If our number one goal is making disciples, then every believer we impact should be empowered to pass the twelvefold test of discipleship reflecting the commitment of the early church while cultivating an apostolic culture!

1. True discipleship begins when we choose to embrace _____.
2. Converts walk where _____ _____, while disciples walk where _____ _____.
3. A convert sets his own _____, while a disciple embraces God's _____.
4. Converts often reject a _____ _____, while disciples accept it.
5. Converts use faith to _____ _____, while disciples use it to _____ _____.
6. Converts are oblivious to _____, while disciples discern it.
7. Disciples volunteer for _____, while converts hesitate.
8. Disciples dare not covenant with _____, but converts do it repeatedly.
9. Disciples are vigilant about who their actions _____, but converts are not.
10. Disciples escape financial manipulation because they give only by _____ need, while converts usually respond to _____ need.
11. Disciples display the _____ _____ _____ _____, while converts do not.
12. Disciples have to extend _____, while converts think it is optional.

To place an order, contact

Web site: www.wordatwork.org

"Word At Work" Ministries
P.O. Box 366
Placentia, CA 92871 USA

(714)693-3033
Fax: (714)693-7848

E-mail: wordatwork@sbcglobal.net

ABOUT THE AUTHOR

Al Houghton grew up in a small town in Missouri. He graduated from the University of Missouri at Columbia with a Bachelor of Science degree in Marketing. After graduation he joined the United States Navy to become a pilot, flying 161 combat reconnaissance missions during the Vietnam War. He left the military to fly commercially, but God dramatically intervened calling him into ministry.

In 1975 he moved to Southern California to attend seminary and earned a Master of Divinity degree in Theology. Immediately upon graduation, the Lord instructed him to start a teaching ministry and live by faith.

The teaching ministry began in home Bible studies, but grew to occupy other facilities, like Mott Auditorium on the campus of the U.S. Center for World Missions in Pasadena, where Al taught for ten years.

1984–87 marked a transition as the Lord began speaking about local churches being centers for future Holy Spirit outpourings. Al dedicated his ministry to building the body of Christ and prefers to minister to local churches, where he can impart his prophetic teaching gift and bring the meat of God's Word.

A daily bible study, entitled "Word At Work" was begun in 1981. It is still published monthly and available upon request or may be downloaded at www.wordatwork.org.

Other CD series are available online through www.wordatwork.org. A DVD series encouraging and defining selective biblical aids to the application of "Sure Mercy" will be announced online.

Al's other books, *Converts or Disciples?*, *Marked Men* and *Purifying the Altar* can be obtained online at www.wordatwork.org The original publication of *Purifying the Altar* may be downloaded in English or Spanish.